BREAD MACHINE

COOKBOOK

A Complete Baking Guide with Recipes for Making Bread at Home Even if You are a Beginner. A Cooking Technique for a Tasty Meal

Melissa Pot

TABLE OF CONTENTS

Introduction

The popularity of homemade bread is growing every day around the world. People are choosing to bake their own bread, mainly due to the health reasons. In coming years, we will most likely observe a growing demand for homemade bread baking.
I want to be the tiny part of this movement and activity
therefore, I have decided to publish this cookbook with delicious bread machine recipes for homemade bread which are perfect for healthy lifestyle followers. The recipes in this book are simple to prepare and bake.

This bread baking cookbook is written not only for people that are choosing a healthier lifestyle, but also for people who want to try new tastes and experiences in bread baking.

Most of the bread recipes from this book are simple to bake. Moreover, homemade bread is cheaper and healthier if we compare it with the bread we buy in shops. I would like to encourage you to test those recipes and to experiment, not always strictly following the recipes given, but adding your own flavors and tastes!

It is often said that "cooking is an art whilst baking is a science" - and not a truer word was said. Baking requires a chemical reaction, which changes the components whilst being baked. The exact measurements and ratios must be correct to get the best outcome...in other words it's an exact science.

The good news is you needn't be an artist or a scientist to make a great loaf of bread in your bread machine. It is however helpful to understand the basis of the bio-chemical process which magically makes bread.

One of the key ingredients of most bread making is yeast. Yeast is a type of fungus made up of single cells, which reproduce and can convert sugar into alcohol and carbon dioxide. Carbon dioxide is what gives bread its light, airy texture while the alcohol, when cooked and burned off, gives bread its distinctive flavor.

Yeast when added to flour and water causes a chemical reaction. Starch that is present in flour is turned into a type of sugar called maltose. This process is what makes the bread rise by producing carbon dioxide. The addition of more sugar to a recipe will help this process further, but too much will spoil it.

Yeast is an organism, which becomes more active in warmer temperatures. This is why in a traditional hand-prepared loaf the bread dough is placed in a warm oven to react faster.

Wheat flour, when mixed with water, forms the dough which becomes elastic in its texture when kneaded. This is because the kneading process of the flour and water releases a protein known as gluten. Gluten allows the bread to capture the carbon dioxide produced by the yeast giving a light, spongy loaf (look at the air bubbles you can see when breaking a fresh loaf of bread).

This is why it is so important to be accurate with your measurements. Each recipe lists the correct ratio of ingredients in relation to each other to make the chemical reaction (science) just right.

Similarly, the sequence of adding ingredients to your bread machine is equally important. For example, yeast when in contact with water will begin activating too early and can become ineffective if it comes into direct contact with salt and sugar before the mixing cycle begins. This is why we list the ingredients in specific order i.e. starting with water and generally ending with yeast. Altering the sequence of ingredients will affect how your loaf turns out.

Luckily for us the bread machine makes the amazing chemical process very easy. All we have to do is adhere carefully to the measurements, set the cycle and wait for the machine to make a perfect homemade loaf.

Chapter 1 History of Bread

Making bread is a great activity, has a potential calming effect, and most importantly, provides the deep inner satisfaction of serving warm homemade bread for your family.

It is incredible how just a few simple ingredients produce such a wonderful delight and almost magical food.

Bread making is a skill that not too many even skilled chefs master completely. It really takes time to create artisan loaves, and usually that process, for the chefs, starts very early in the morning.

On the other side, in our everyday world and outside professional kitchens, many people know how to make great loaves, but unfortunately, do not have time. The most natural solution is to go out and buy bread, but in most cases, they are just rounded pale blobs, without interesting flavor or texture.

Luckily, thanks to bread machines, the process of bread making is simplified, and even in the hectic world, we are living today, serving rich and delicious bread is entirely possible.

The bread machine allows you to make all kinds of bread, including:

White bread
Sweet bread
Vegetable bread
Meat bread
Spicy bread

This book will give you a complete understanding of bread as a food and bread making machines, and teach you how to make all kind of bread types.

A bread machine does it all instead of you. This means you will be able to avoid kitchen mess as the bread machine does everything from mixing to kneading, and baking. Yes, it sounds like magic, but it is really. Just imagine warm bread and a clean kitchen. Dreams can come true!

Bread machines keep your allergies under control. By this, we mean that you can choose the ingredients you want and create a bread that is allergen-free and one that will not cause any harm to your body. This feature is very appreciated by those who are gluten-intolerant or have issues with yeast infections. You can make your own bread that is way better than the store-bought version, at a low cost, and, you know it is created in a clean environment where cross-contamination is not possible.

A bread machine allows you to have fresh, warm bread every day. This is perhaps the most obvious benefit of a bread making machine. Most bread machines have a time function you can set to have your bread ready at a certain time. This is very useful as you can prepare the ingredients and then continue with your daily chores, while the bread machine does everything else for you. Just imagine, you are coming home from an exhausting day of work, and warm, delicious bread is waiting for you!

Bread machines save money. Yes, bread machines may be expensive initially, but buying bread every day, or even just every week, is more expensive. Not to mention all of that thrown away bread, the stale bread that no one wants to eat anymore. With each slice, you are throwing away your money. The bread machine maker allows you to make smaller or larger loaves and ones that fit your family's dietary and consumption habits. Besides, making bread from scratch is always cheaper than buying it at the store.

Bread machines produce better bread quality. Fresh bread is fresh bread, and no store-bought version can compete with that. Also, what about that chewy, rubber-like bread you sometimes get? Something like that will never happen to you with a bread making machine. The homemade bread is made with natural ingredients and does not have any additives. The additives which are used in store-bought bread can keep it fresher for a longer time, but they affect the texture. So, it is always better to make bread fresh and additive-free, than to eat "fake-fresh" bread for days.

Bread machines are easy to use. The bread machine looks like a simple appliance, and believe us, it is. If you are not good with the baking process and somehow you always end up with over- or under-cooked foods, you can skip this worry as the bread making machine bakes it all to the perfection.

Bread making machines make more than bread - the bread machine can be used for many other purposes instead of making bread. You can use it to make jams, pasta, and even pizza dough. The possibilities are endless.
Before we start talking about bread machines, let's pause for a moment and talk about bread itself. Experts aren't sure when humans first figured out how bake bread, and new evidence suggests we actually

made bread before we started farming the wheat and oats. Currently, the oldest bread ever discovered is 14,000 years old. We began farming wheat for bread around 8,000 B.C.E. and ground it into flour first using rocks, and then with a mortar and pestle. Around 800 B.C.E., the first mill with flat, spinning stones appears, with steel taking over much later in the mid 1800's C.E.

As for yeast, bakers used to wait for the bacteria to show up naturally. Once their bread dough was made, they could also save a bit of it, which still contained yeast, and use it for the other loaf. Humans also figured out that yeast could be found in beer foam. In the late 18th-century C.E., commercial yeast was developed, making baking much easier for everyone.

To bake bread, you need heat. The first ovens come from Asia and were made from clay, though some kind of structure that trapped heat has been present in just about every civilization. The first "modern" oven made from bricks and tiles originated in France. In the 18th century, Germany began producing cast-iron ovens, and as 1900 drew closer, the first version of an electric oven popped up in the Windsor Hotel in Ottawa, Canada. In 1954, the first microwave oven launched. What about the bread machine? Panasonic released the first one-loaf bread-making machine designed for the home in 1986. Big commercial bread-making machines that kneaded dough and performed other tasks existed before then, but the home baker was doing everything by hand. The home bread maker required a year of research by project engineers, a software developer, and a baker. Together, they created an automatic machine equipped with special "ribs" that imitated how to knead dough. By the 1990's, the Panasonic bread maker was popular all over the world, including the United States.

Chapter 2 Bread Machine Overview

Making bread can be extremely satisfying, but it is often also extremely time-consuming. In fact, some bread takes many hours to make, and most of that time is spent waiting for the bread to rise. In many cases, if the bread is not kneaded and left to rise at the right time, you may end up with dry or deflated bread, and all of that hard work may seem like a total waste. If you have a busy schedule, it is almost impossible to find time to make bread, especially if you are running errands all day. Bread machines are the perfect tools to give you those wonderful loaves without lifting a finger.

The key to good bread comes from its machines. Whether you are new to bread machines or you have been using them for years, there is always space for a new bread machine. Some of the best bread machines on the market have a wide variety of options to accommodate any loaf, but not every machine fits in every budget. When looking for a quality bread machine, find something that works without much assistance but offers the right heat and mixing capabilities. Assuming you are new to bread machines, it can seem overly complicated and overwhelming to find a machine that fits within those criteria.

The introduction of bread makers or bread machines made it possible for more people to bake bread at home. This is done in a faster way than usual and you can easily do it even though you haven't tried doing something like this before. All you need is a handy machine, which is now available in various models, sizes, and brands. The dough will still go through the usual process of kneading, rising, and all that, but this time, you can leave the machine as it works on your bread and come back when it's done.

So how do you use a bread machine? First, place the appliance on a counter near an outlet. Do not plug it yet.

Check if the lid will open easily without hitting any other tools or cabinets in the kitchen. Remove the baking pan. Wash it with gentle soap, rinse thoroughly and let it dry before using.

Place the kneading blade to plan and set it aside. Follow the recipe for the bread you are making.

Place the baking pan in the machine, close the lid, plug it in, and choose the right settings based on the recipe you're doing.

Press the Start/Stop button to begin the bread making process.

Note that there are certain recipes wherein you'll be required to raise the lid during the process to add certain ingredients, such as fruits and nuts. There are also certain brands that have an automatic fruit and nut dispenser feature.

It is important to use the exact measurement of each ingredient in the recipe. The yeast must not come into contact with liquid during the preparation process. You must first make a small well at the center of the ingredients in the pan using your hand where you will put the yeast.

When it comes to settings, the basic types found in many bread machines include the following:

Basic or White setting lasts for 3 hours. This is used in many recipes because it creates the best results among all the other settings.

The Whole wheat setting lasts for 3 hours and 40 minutes. The duration is longer than the basic setting because bread with more than 50 percent whole wheat flour needs longer time to rise.

The French setting lasts for 3 hours and 50 minutes. French bread has a heartier crust that needs longer time to knead, rise, and bake.

The Sweet setting lasts for 2 hours and 50 minutes. This is used for recipes with lots of proteins fats, and sugar.

The Dough setting lasts for 1 hour and 30 minutes. This is used in preparing dough for specialty bread and rolls that you will later shape using your hands, leave to rise, and bake in an oven.

The Bake setting lasts for 1 hour and is used in making jams or dough. There are also models with the Express bake feature that you can use in baking bread in less than an hour or 80 minutes for larger loaves.

Another button that you need to set is the crust color button. Your choice depends on your personal preference. L is for light, P is for medium, and H is for dark. The names of the settings may vary depending on the model of the machine you are using but basically have similar functions.

There are some models that have a designated setting for loaf size. In this case, you simply have to choose the size based on the recipe you're making.

Once you have placed the baking pan inside the machine with all the ingredients as per the recipe, it will go through various processes that you can see at its dedicated viewing window. Once the timer starts, the machine will knead the dough for the first 10 minutes.

The dough will rise for 20 minutes before the machine kneads it for the second time for 15 minutes. The dough will rise again for 20 minutes and excess air is punched down for 30 seconds. The dough will have 55 minutes for its final rise before it begins to bake for the next 60 minutes.

Once the process is done, all you have to do is carefully lift the pan, turn it upside down to get the bread out and leave it for a couple of minutes to cool. If the kneading blade comes out with the bread, remove it using a plastic utensil but be careful because it is also hot. After 15 minutes, you can slice the bread and serve.

The process is easy once you get the hang of it. Make sure that you read the manual that comes with the machine and start practicing the process of bread making.

Chapter 3 Bread Making Equipment

S everal tools can aid you in pulling the best texture and flavorful homemade bread.

1.Baking pans
Purchase baking pans in different shapes to give a specific shape to loaves.

2.Loaf pan
Loaf pans are made of disposable aluminum foil, heavy-gauge aluminum, ceramic material or Pyrex glass. It comes in a rectangle shape.

3.Baking sheet
You will need a few baking sheets in different sizes, depending on the size of the dough and oven. Purchase baking sheets that won't warp at high temperatures, such as gauge aluminum or steel. Standard sizes of baking sheets are 10.5 by 15 inches with a raised 1-inch edge, half baking sheet and quarter sheet pan.

4.Bread mills
You enjoy fresh flour in your bread by milling wheat in your bread mill.

5.Cooling rack
A wire cooling rack helps in cooling down the bread properly after baking is done. Purchase the one that has short legs and allow adequate circulation.

6.Food processor or stand mixer
Although the preferable way to mix ingredients for the dough is by hand, it can be a messy procedure. Plus, it is difficult to work with sticky hands. Therefore, if you are baking regularly, combine ingredients in a food processor or stand mixer with a dough hook. These machines make the mixing process more manageable and they are reliable to turn out an edible dough.

7.Knives
A sharp knife can make cuts on the dough, such as in hot cross buns. Also, purchase a serrated knife for slicing the bread. Always cut bread

on a cutting board to make a cut in the loaf with no damage to the knife.

8.Measuring cups and spoons
You must have cups and spoons for accurate measurement of the dry and wet ingredients for the dough. A long wooden spoon will also work in place of plastic spoons. Purchase clear liquid measuring cups that come with a spout to accurately pour liquid ingredients.

9.Mixing bowls
You must have a sturdy large bowl, about 4-quarts, on hand to mix your ingredients. Use a plastic or ceramic bowl in various sizes for mixing.

10.Plastic spatula
This tool will help in removing stuck dough on the inside of the bowl or bread machine pans. You can also use a spatula to transfer dough by lifting it.

11.Plastic wrap/kitchen towel
A plastic wrap or a linen kitchen towel is used while the dough is expanding. The kitchen towel should be damp, not moist, and plastic wrap should be sprayed with oil.

12.Parchment paper
Parchment paper is used to line baking pans and loaf pans before adding dough in it as it cuts down cleaning the baking and loaf pans. Grease parchment paper when using.

13.Pastry brushes
Pastry brushes are used to grease dough with oil or butter or applying glazes. A silicone pastry brush works best, and it is easy to clean.

14.Pastry board
If your kitchen counter is not good enough for rolling the dough, then you can consider a pastry board for this job. It is made of bamboo, wood, or marble. Purchase the pastry board that can lock to your working table or kitchen counter.

15.Rolling pin
A rolling pin helps in rolling and shaping the dough in appropriate shape and thickness.

16. Silicone mat

If you are frustrated with cutting the parchment paper to the right size for baking, you can use a silicon mat as an alternative. They come in sizes of half and full sheet baking trays and are reusable and easy to clean. They also prevent sticking of baking items to the tray.

17. Timer

Timing is everything in bread baking. A timer will let you relax throughout the baking process and will indicate when the dough is ready. So, with the timer, you don't have to keep an eye on the clock continuously for noting the time and monitor the progress of dough.

18. Thermometer

Temperature is a significant factor when baking bread with yeast. You must know the accurate temperature of the water and the environment to achieve the best result of fermentation. For this, purchase a quality digital probe thermometer or a long-stemmed instant-read yeast thermometer.

19. Whisker

A whisker is a very handy tool in mixing ingredients. Use a stainless steel or silicone wire whiskers with a long handle when making bread.

20. Cheese Grater

Pizza is a delicious dish, and we all would agree it would not be the same without cheese on it. Cheese is a staple ingredient for pizza making, and when speaking about the cheese, it cannot be used in large slices on the pizza. To get your cheese perfectly grated, use stainless-steel cheese graters. They will perfectly grate the cheese and make it properly prepared for use on pizza. Besides grating the cheese, you can grate some other ingredients as well, like salami or bell peppers.

21. Kitchen Scale

A kitchen scale is a must-have kitchen tool. Preparing certain types of food without one is practically impossible. Yes, there are cups, but when it comes to dough-based meals, a kitchen scale is necessary equipment. The best example is bread, which is hard to make without a kitchen scale. The reason behind it is because flour is a compressible, and measurement in cups will sometimes just not be accurate. To get your bread dough perfect, we suggest you use kitchen scales. You can find classic and digital ones, but for the best accuracy, choose digital scales. They are so much easier to use, and most of them have very modern and exciting designs.

Chapter 4 Differences of Bread Machines

A bread machine is a multi-functional kitchen appliance or device that is built for bread baking. The device performs the function of mixing, kneading and baking. It comes with a bread pan with in-built paddles, located in the middle of a multi-function oven.

Familiarize yourself with the machine. Inspect all the machine components, the machine comes with a hinged lid, you can easily lift and shut. It comes with a control panel with various buttons. When you open the machine, you will find a bucket or pan, the bread pan function as a mixing bowl and a baking pan. Inside the center of the bread pan, you will find a kneading blade or bread paddle. The kneading blade functions to mix and knead the dough.

Familiarize yourself with the machine settings. Start by observing the display screen and buttons on the control panel. You will find on the select button the Start/Stop button, Timer and Crust Color. You will find several bread kneading and baking choices-Sweet, Whole Wheat, low carb, French, White or Basic, Rapid, & Dough.

Know your bread pan capacity. A simple method to measure your bread pan capacity is by pouring water into the bucket using a cup measurement. Count how many cups of water it takes to fill up the bread bucket.

Less than 10 cups capacity will bake 1 pounds loaf of bread in the pan
10 cups capacity will bake 1-1/2 pound loaves of bread in the pan
More than 12 cups or more capacity will bake 2 pound loaves of bread. This process is really important, so measure carefully. If you try and bake a 2 lb recipe in a 1 lb machine, it may come out a big mess.

Before you add your ingredients into the bread machine pan, first, you remove the machine pan, insert the kneading paddle and add your ingredients according to machine instructions or your recipe instructions.

Next, Place the pan in the bread machine, close the lid of the bread pan and set the program you wish through the machine panel.

Afterwards, the kneading process starts, you will hear the sounds. If you machine is the one that comes with a viewing window, you will be able to see the whole kneading process.

This is the next phase that ushers in the rising phase. The machine will be quiet and allow the dough rise for some time during this rising phase. After which there will be a second phase of kneading and proving.

The Final stage is the baking.

Basic cycle
It has an average time of 3 hours to 4 hours, this setting is great for most savory yeast breads with most simple bread recipes, I use this setting for my baking most of the time.

Sweet
This cycle is meant to prepare and bake sweet yeast breads with high sugar or fat content. This cycle requires lower baking temperature to prevent a burned crust. Choose this setting for recipes that call for cheese or eggs.

Quick bread or cake cycle
This cycle is for bread that does not require yeast, simple cake recipes or quick bread mixes. The baking time varies from machine to machine.

Whole wheat cycle
This setting requires longer time for dough to knead and rise. Choose this setting for recipes that include cereal, or whole-grain flours, you can make good texture whole wheat/grain loaves with this setting. .

Raisin/nut cycle
Some bread machine comes with Raisin/nut cycle
this setting allows you to add dried fruits or nuts in the kneading process at an audibly signal, such as a beep, just in time to incorporate lightly with the dough.

French cycle
French breads setting takes longer time to rise on most machines and a slightly higher baking temperature because they have little or no sugar. This cycle can help you attain the crust and texture that are similar to that of Italian and French breads. I mostly use this cycle for breads that have little or no sugar or fat.

Rapid cycle
This is a bread machine setting for bread in a rush. The cycle can run for 30 minutes to 2 hours, it varies from machine to machine.

Dough cycle
This is a bread machine setting that allows you to withdraw the dough before baking commences, you can shape dough in flatbreads, pizza

crusts, rolls, breadsticks or add your fillings. These breads are finished off in conventional oven.

Jam cycle

The jam cycle is perfect for making simple homemade fruit spread. The bread machine is turned into a veritable saucepan
it takes care of the mixing and cooking for 1 to 1 1/2 hours.

Delay cycle

This setting allows you program the machine to complete the cycle up to 24 hours later after you have added the ingredients. Note that this cycle is not recommended for perishable ingredients, such as eggs, milk, cheese or butter.

Chapter 5 Advantages of a bread machine and the difference of kneading by hand

Bread machines make bread baking easier and help with the bread baking process.

A bread machine will make almost everything instead of you

Bread machines can mix or knead the dough so there is no need to do it yourself. The baking process is also painless. You just need to spoon the dough into the bread machine, close the lid and turn the bread machine on the proper bread program. There will be no dirty dishes and your kitchen will stay clean.

Owning a bread machine is a great advantage for your busy lifestyle as it not only saves time in the kitchen but also makes your life better in many ways.

Fresh Bread Anytime

Traditional oven baking is not so much a single task as a series of steps. It requires careful planning to get baked bread out of your oven. Of course you can purchase bread from your local bakery, but it's not always freshly baked. With a bread machine, you do not have to plan in advance as all you need to do is add the ingredients and start the machine. You can enjoy freshly baked bread anytime you want it.

Ingredient Freedom

You don't have any choice as to the ingredients in commercially available breads. With a bread machine, you can customize the taste and texture of your breads because you have the freedom to add your favorite fruits, spices, herbs, cheese and so on and enjoy your choice of flavors.

Effortless and Clutter less

Traditional bread making makes lots of mess what with all the mixing and kneading. A bread machine creates no mess at all, as everything from mixing to baking is done within the bread pan.

Healthy & Economical

When you add up the cost of store-bought bread over the years, a bread machine is a much more economical choice. More importantly, it is a smart way to enjoy freshly baked bread with healthy ingredients as you can choose the flour and everything else that goes into it.

Your bread is always warm, crispy and fresh

This is perhaps one of the most important factors of having a bread machine and baking bread at home. You can choose the time when you want your bread to be ready by setting a time function most bread machines will have. This is a very useful function because you can forget about the bread and continue with your daily routine, but the bread will be there on time. You are coming home after a hard day, but crispy, delicious and warm bread is waiting for you there!

You can control the ingredients in your bread
You can choose only "healthy" ingredients because when you bake at home you always know what ingredients you want to add to your bread. Only you decide what ingredients to choose and bake the bread that will be allergen free and won't be harmful to your body.
Baking bread at home saves your money and family budget
Buying bread every day could be very painful to your budget, especially when you have a big family. Well, bread machines aren't cheap, but buying bread every day or every few days would be more expensive. Moreover, bread machine allows you to choose the size of the bread loaves. You can make your bread portions bigger or smaller. Buying all the ingredients and baking bread at home is always cheaper than buying it at the stores.

Quality of your bread will be always better
The chewy and rubber-like bread sounds familiar, right? Well with homemade bread you can forget about that problem. Store-bought bread couldn't compete with homemade bread, because your bread will be always fresh. Your bread will not have any additives and will be made with natural only ingredients. Due to harmful additives in store-bought bread, such as L-cysteine, potassium bromate, high fructose corn syrup, and many others it will stay "fake fresh" for a long period of time.

Bread machines are simple and easy to use
If your problem is overcooked food with bake machine you can forget about that problem, because it will always bake your bread perfectly.

Bread machines are multipurpose
Bread machines could be used not only for baking bread but also for preparing other types of food. With the bread machine, you can prepare meat, pasta, vegetables and a lot of other dishes.
Kneading is the process of freeing up the dough, especially the gluten present, and allow for air spaces as you may desire. It's not a complicated process at all. Here is how I do mine. I will press down on the dough firmly with both palms of my hands, and fold the dough

in half, press again, turn the dough towards ninety degrees, press down once more and repeat the process. When you notice it has begun sticking to your hands or the smooth board, you add more flour to it. In this process, I see myself picking the dough, passing it on my shoulder, and smacking it over the wooden surface. do this for about ten times until the mixture is well stretched.

When you plan on making French bread, there is a need to keep it wet. Dip your hands in water or sprinkle some water depending on the largeness of the holes you want to see.

Over kneading rarely occurs when you are working on it this way. If you have machines, the process may be faster, and there may arise a time when it truly reaches a point of over kneading. At this point, the bread flour breaks. I have never been able to achieve such an end using my hands.

Chapter 6 Tools for making bread

The tools required for baking are very versatile and depends on what your specific domain in baking is or how your recipes are being prepped. But there are certain tools which are being utilized more than often. They are somewhat like 'basic' tools required for baking purposes in your kitchen ranging from stirring cookies to baking a cake. These tools are considered to be present before you kick off your baking session.

1.Spoons and Measuring Cups (Both Dry and Liquid)
The art of baking is based upon measurements and the right proportions. This is why you are always going to need measuring cups and spoons for drafting the right proportions of ingredients for your recipes. And you can't just rely on a single measuring cup, rather you will need both liquid and dry measuring cups for baking almost any recipe. Keep these measuring cups in a convenient place so that they can be quickly reached without any hindrance as they are used extensively in almost all baking recipes.
Almost all measuring spoons have a set of a teaspoon, tablespoon, ¼ teaspoon, and ½ teaspoon. In addition to this, all measuring cups are available in sets of sizes ranging in the following manner, i.e. one cup, ½ cup, 1/3 cup, and ¼ cup. In case of liquid measuring cups, you can go on with a 1-cup sized cup but it is more convenient to have 2-cup and 3-cup sized measuring cups too in your closet.

2.Wooden Spoons
Although it is enough to have a single wooden spoon, it is preferred for you to have more than a single wooden spoon so that in case of loss or any damage, you have alternative options. They are the best option for stirring as they are sturdy and can be easily used in even the thickest possible doughs. Always hand washes them after usage so that they don't get cracked.

3.Rubber Spatula / Scraper
Rubber scraper is also one of the most used tools in baking. It is best used for the scrapping of the last bit of the batter or the dough out of the pan or even for scrapping off all the crannies and nooks of the jar. They are also best in usage for folding together both dry and wet ingredients. For your convenience, we should let you know that silicone scrapers are more heat resistant than rubber ones.

4.Spatula / Metal Turner

Spatulas are good or transferring freshly baked cookies into a cooling rack or even for taking a piece out of a cake of a larger pan.it is preferred that you have a spatula that is having a thinner metal blade in it. This will make it easy in movements while sliding it down anything without the fear of curbing the cookies or squishing the dough.

5.Pastry Brush

This tool is way too versatile in its usage and that is why it is falling into the 'must-have' category. You can grease your pan before pouring the batter of the cake, or coating dough with egg wash or melted butter or even in painting milk on the top of the piecrust. It is highly recommended for those who do baking frequently.

6.Whisk

Apart from being effective in beating together with a few eggs, the wire whisk is useful in various other baking operations too. It is also best to be used in properly mixing together various dry ingredients. You can also use it to effectively stir your homemade custard.

7.Kitchen Scissors

Kitchen scissors are an important part of almost every kitchen operation and are not just confined to baking only. You can use it in cutting parchments for fitting them in a pan, sipping off a few herbs, or even for cutting open various packages and jars, etc.

8.Rolling Pin

Apart from rolling out puff pastry, cookie dough, and piecrusts, rolling pins are used in various other procedures in the kitchen. Like you can use it for crushing various ingredients by putting them in a sealable bag and rolling them over and over in case you don't have a food processor available. Rolling pins can make your crushing procedures very easy and handy.

9.Fine-Mesh Sieve

A sieve can work in various ways depending upon how you are using it. In case of baking, it is very essentially used in adding a dusting of powdered sugar to a freshly finished pan of cookies or brownies. It can be also used for sifting up various dry ingredients. It is also useful in draining out wet ingredients like quinoa which are too small for a regular colander and are easy to slip off of it.

10. Chef's Knife

This is the all in one type of knife and if you have it in your kitchen, you don't need any other knife at all. This is much like an all-purpose knife and is best in use for dicing, mincing, chopping, and slicing, for almost any ingredients that are involved in your recipes.

11. Paring Knife

This small knife is best in use for coring and peeling foods like apples and that is why it is must in your drawer for recipes like apple pie. It is best to be used for foods which are too delicate and can't be chopped or sliced with a Chef's knife.

12. Rectangular Baking Pan

The size of a rectangular baking pan is 13 x 9 x 2 inches and is must in your inventory. You can utilize the pan for many sweet recipes like cookie bars, brownies, and cakes, etc. apart from this, it can be used for many other savory uses too. This is the ultimate best option for having a baking pan in your kitchen.

13. Round Cake Pan

These are best for towering cakes and should be more than one as a single round cake pan isn't going to be sufficient for various recipes. They are available in both 8 inches and 9 inches size, but you have to make it sure that you have two of them in the same size for making a perfect towering cake.

14. Loaf Pan

Zucchini bread, pumpkin bread, and banana bread, all of these homemade breads require a loaf pan. It is also best for making a yeast bread at your home. You will need two of them in your inventory for perfect baking.

15. Pie Plate

Of course, a pie plate is used for making the sweetest apple pies but it has many there uses to it as well. You can use it for making various other desserts too with the pie plate. It also has a lot of savory pies like taco pies and meatball pies for dinner, in addition to frozen icebox pies too.

16. Square Baking Pan

A square baking pan is used for making desserts in a smaller quantity instead of making a chunk of them. Brownies, cornbread, cakes, and cookie bars, which you can serve up on a square pan of sizes 8 x 8 or 9 x 9 inches.

17. Wire Rack

If you want to avoid overbaked, soggy cakes and cookies for your dessert, you have to ensure that you have a wire rack in your inventory. This instrument allows smooth circulation of air around baked food when they are cooling down. This makes it taste the same at room temperature as it was when it was taken out fresh from the oven.

18. Muffin Rack

A muffin rack is best to be used for making muffins for birthday bashes or brunch. It has various savory uses too like in preparing mini meatloaves, meatballs, and pizza cups, etc.

19. Cookie Sheet

Although a single cookie sheet can work fine, having two of them in your kitchen can make your baking much easy. Although, as evident from the name, it can be used for making any kind of cookies you can also use it in recipes that involve sheet pan.

20. Hand Mixer / Stand Mixer

Although it is not necessary to have a fancy stand mixer in your kitchen a hand mixer is a must in your baking inventory for perfect baking. It is perfect for mixing up batters and doughs as it makes them pretty easier. In addition to this, it is also the best approach to mix various ingredients into a stiff, tough cookie dough without exerting out much energy or force.

21. Parchment Paper

If you were already missing out on a parchment paper, grab it ASAP! Placing a parchment paper on your pan before baking your recipes will not only make your cleaning easier but also restrict the food from getting stuck to the pan. You can also go for a bit expensive silicone baking mats that are reusable, but the best option is still the parchment paper.

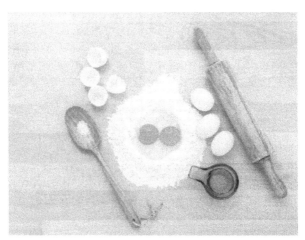

Chapter 7 The essential ingredients for the dough

Salt

A little amount of salt is basic for bread making. It builds up the mixture and gives enhance. Utilize fine table salt or ocean salt as opposed to coarse ground salt which is best kept for sprinkling over hand-molded moves and so forth to give a crunchy surface. Low salt substitutes are best evaded as most don't contain sodium. Salt fortifies the gluten structure and makes the mixture increasingly flexible. Salt restrains the development of yeast from averting over-rising and stops the mixture crumbling. Take care to include the right sum as a lot of salt will slaughter the yeast or counteract it rising adequately.

Sweeteners

Utilize white or darker sugars, nectar, malt separate, brilliant syrup, maple syrup, molasses or treacle.

- Sugar and fluid sugars help with the shade of the bread and add a brilliant shading to the outside layer.
- Sugar draws in dampness which improves the keeping nature of the bread.
- Sugar nourishes the yeast. It isn't basic as present-day sorts of dried yeast can benefit from the natural sugars and starches found in the flour yet it will make the batter increasingly dynamic.
- Sweetbreads have a moderate dimension of sugar with the organic product, coating or icing including additional sweetness. Utilize the SWEET program for these bread.

If substituting a fluid sugar for sugar then the all-out fluid amount of the formula should be diminished marginally.

Fats and oils

A little measure of fat or oil will give a gentler scrap and expands the freshness of the portion. Use spread, margarine or fat in little amounts. Try not to utilize low-fat spreads as they contain up to 40% water and can influence the general amounts in your formula.

Liquid

Some type of fluid is basic. Typically water or milk is utilized. Water gives a crisper outcome than milk. Water can be joined with skimmed milk powder. In the event that utilizing the time defer it is imperative to utilize water and skimmed milk powder as common milk will break down whenever left to represent excessively long. For most projects, you can utilize water straight from the tap yet if utilizing the ULTRA QUICK projects it should be tepid.

- On extremely cool days measure the water and leave to remain at room temperature for 30 minutes before use.
- If utilizing milk, don't utilize it straight from the ice chest, abandon it to remain at room temperature for 30 minutes before use.
- Buttermilk, yogurt, harsh cream and delicate cheeses, for example, Ricotta, bungalow or fromage frais would all be able to be utilized as a feature of the fluid substance and will give an increasingly damp and delicate scrap.
- Eggs can be added to the mixture to enhance it. Eggs improve the shading and help to add structure and soundness to the gluten amid rising. If you are utilizing eggs, lessen the fluid substance likewise. Spot the egg in the estimating container and top up with fluid to the right dimension for the formula.

Yeast

- For best outcomes utilize a simple mix, quick activity yeast.
- Use just the measure of yeast-expressed in the formula. If an excessive amount of is included it will make the mixture spill out absurd of the bread skillet.
- Once a sachet of yeast is opened it ought to be utilized inside 48 hours.
- Always use yeast before its utilization by date.
- You may likewise discover dried yeast that has been extraordinarily intended for use in bread producers. Continuously adhere to the guidelines on the parcel.

- On extremely chilly days let the water from the tap remain at room temperature for 30 minutes before use. In like manner for fixings from the refrigerator.
- Use every one of the fixings at room temperature and water from cold except if expressed generally in the
- Add the fixings to the bread container in the request proposed in the formula. Keep the yeast dry and separate from some other fluids added to the container, until blending starts.
- Accurate estimating is fundamental for an effective portion. Pursue either metric or magnificent estimations, don't blend the two. Utilize the estimating container and spoon provided or utilize precise kitchen scales.
- Always utilize crisp fixings, inside their utilization by date. Transitory fixings, for example, milk, cheddar, vegetables, and crisp organic products may crumble, particularly in warm conditions. These should just be utilized in bread which is made right away.

Do not include an excessive amount of fat as it shapes an obstruction between the yeast and flour, hindering the activity of the yeast, which could give an overwhelming, thick portion.

Cut margarine and different fats into little pieces before adding to the bread skillet.

Giving the working or a light covering of oil may make it simpler to expel on the off chance that it prepares into the portion.

Chapter 8 Techniques used in the preparation of bread

When you are using a bread machine for the first time, it's common to have some concerns. However, they are quite easy to fix. The following are some useful tips and quick-and-easy fixes for the most common problems encountered while baking bread in a bread machine.

Dough Check
You can check the progress of the dough while the bread machine is mixing the ingredients. Take a quick check after 5 minutes of kneading. An ideal dough with the right amount of dry and wet ingredients makes one smooth ball and feels slightly tacky. You can open the lid to evaluate the dough. Do not worry about interfering with the kneading process by opening the lid
the bread structure won't be affected even if you poke it to get a feel for the dough.
If the dough feels too wet/moist or does not form into a ball shape, you can add 1 tablespoon of flour at a time and check again after a few minutes. If you feel that the dough is too dry, or it has formed two or three small balls, you can add 1 teaspoon of water at a time and check again after a few minutes.

Fruit/Nut Bread
When making fruit or nut breads, it is very important to add the fruits or nuts at the right time. Not all bread machines come with a nut/fruit dispenser or hopper. If yours doesn't have one, don't worry
the machine will signal you with a beep series when it's time to add the fruits or nuts.
Citrus Ingredients
Citrus ingredients such as lemon zest, orange zest, orange juice, lemon juice and pineapple juice can create issues with yeast fermentation if added in excess. Do not add more than the quantity specified in a recipe. The same goes for alcohol and cinnamon.

Salt Adjustment
When making small loaves (around 1 pound), sometimes the loaf rises more or less than expected. In many such instances, the issue is with the quantity of salt added. To avoid problems, try using less salt or cutting back on the quantity specified in the recipe. Using sea salt or coarse salt can also help prevent problems with small loaves.

Bread Collapse

The amount of yeast is very important for proper rising. The most common reason for bread collapse during the baking process is adding too much or too little yeast. Do not add more yeast than specified in the recipe. Also check the expiration date on the yeast pack freshly packed yeast provides the best results. Other reasons for bread collapse are using cold water and adding excess salt.

Failure to Rise

Many factors can contribute to the failure of a dough to rise completely. Insufficient gluten content, miscalculated ingredients, excess salt, excess sugar, and using cold ingredients are the most common reasons. Always warm any chilled ingredients or place them at room temperature for a while before adding them to the bread pan. However, if you are warming any ingredients in your oven, make sure not to overheat them. They need to be lukewarm, at between 80 and 90°F, and not too hot. Also make sure that the yeast does not come in direct contact with the salt, as this creates problems with rising (that is why yeast is added last).

Texture Troubles

If your bread has a coarse texture, try adding more salt and reducing the amount of liquid.

If your bread looks small and feels dense, try using flour with a higher protein content. Bread flour has a sufficient amount of protein, but slightly denser loaves are common when you use heavier flours such as rye flour and whole wheat flour. Use additional ingredients such as fruits, nuts and vegetables in their specified quantities. Adding too much of such ingredients will make your loaf too heavy, small and dense.

Moist or gummy loaves are less common, but it can happen if you have added too much liquid or used too much sugar. Too much liquid can also result in a doughy center.

If you bread has an un browned top, try adding more sugar. This can also happen if your bread machine has a glass top.

If your loaf has a mushroom top, it is probably due to too much yeast or water. Try reducing the amount of water and/or yeast.

Sometimes a baked loaf has some flour on one side. When you bake another time, try scrapping off any visible flour during the kneading cycle with a rubber spatula.

If your loaf has an overly dark crust, try using the Medium crust setting another time. This also happens if you've added too much sugar and when you fail to take out the bread pan after the end of the baking process. It is always advisable to remove the bread pan right after the process is complete.

If your loaf has a sunken top, it is probably because of using too much liquid or overly hot ingredients. This is also common during humid or warm weather.

Excess Rise
Many times a loaf rises more than expected
the most common reasons are too much yeast, too little salt and using cold water. But also make sure that the capacity of your bread pan is sufficient for the size of loaf you have selected
trying to make a large loaf in a small bread pan will obviously lead to such trouble.

Paddles
After the bread machine completes its baking process the paddles may remain inside the bread loaf. Allow the freshly made bread to cool down and then place it on a cutting board and gently take out the paddles.

Spraying the paddles with a cooking spray before you add the ingredients to the bread pan will make it easier to clean them after the bread is baked.

Cleaning
After you take the baked loaf from the bread pan, do not immerse the pan in water. Rather, fill it with warm soapy water.

Chapter 9 Machine cycles and settings

Features: Cycles and Settings

The owner's manual will familiarize you with the different parts of the machine, some basic DIY steps for removal and replacement of the bread pan and the correct order to add the ingredients in the pan. In addition, the manufacturer will list out the features, also known as the cycles of the machine. The purpose of this list is to inform you of the types of breads that your machine can make and the exact time needed to make a loaf on each of these settings. The manual will also use a chart to tell you how long each cycle lasts. Note that the amount of time for each cycle depends on each brand of machine. The following four cycles are the most common in all machines

Basic

This is also known as Basic Bread, Basic Wheat, Basic Mode, White or Standard bread. This setting is most commonly used for all purposes. The cycle lasts for up to three to four hours, based on your machine and is used for whole-wheat or whole-grain breads and white breads that are made up of more than 50 percent bread flour. You can also use this cycle instead of a French Bread cycle or if your machine doesn't have a French bread cycle. In this Basic cycle, there is sometimes the option for "Quick" or "Rapid." Or your machine can have the options in a separate cycle. On many of the newer models, there's an inbuilt alert that goes off when you need to add any extra ingredients, such as raisins or nuts.

Sweet Bread

This cycle makes doughs with a higher sugar and fat content to rise slower than usual. This Sweet Bread cycle has a longer rise time and a reduced baking temperature, just about 250°F. This is because the crust of the sweet bread will brown faster. The inbuilt indicator in this cycle beeps when it's time to add the extra ingredients to the mix such as chopped glacéed fruit or nuts. Also, many sweetbreads are mixed, shaped in the Dough cycle, and baked in the home oven.

Fruit And Nut

This cycle is also known as the Raisin Mode or Mix Bread cycle. This setting is used when nuts, chocolate chips, seeds or dried fruits are added to the dough. With this method, the extra ingredients are not overmixed or completely blended during the extreme speed of the blade action during the kneading phase of the cycle. Many of the newer models have an audible alert inbuilt as part of the Basic and Whole Wheat cycles, rather than built-in a separate cycle. When the alert sounds, it is time to open the lid and add the extras. But if your machine doesn't have this cycle, you can use the Basic cycle for breads with extra ingredients. When I want to try a different taste or color for my bread, I add extras like onions and nuts at the start of the cycle. That way, it is completely pulverized and disintegrates into dough by the time the kneading action is complete.

Variety
This feature was common on the older models. This cycle runs for about the same amount of time that the Basic cycle runs. It has an indicator beep and also displays the signal to "shape" at the second rise, so the dough can be removed, filled and shaped by hand, and then returned to the baking pan for the final rise and baking. This cycle can also be used for a monkey bread or cinnamon swirl. If your machine does not have this feature, you can get it by programming the Basic cycle, pause to interrupt the cycle after the second rise, remove the dough and shape, then return it to the baking pan and press Start to resume cycle and bake the bread.

Dough
This setting is also known as the Rise or Manual cycle. It is perfect for when you want to mix and rise a dough in the machine, then remove the dough, shape it by hand, and bake it in your oven. The setting with the shortest dough cycle is Toastmaster at 1 hour and 3 minutes with 1 hour, 30 minutes as the average, while the Panasonic brand is the longest cycle at 2 hours, 30 minutes (including Preheat). Doughs that are prepared on this cycle are meant to be shaped into traditional loaves or into special shapes like egg twists, cloverleaf dinner rolls, pizza, breadsticks, croissants, or bagels, and baked in the oven. You can adjust your favorite recipes for this cycle, and using quantities that will fit in your machine. When the alert beeps, remove the dough and follow the instructions in the menu to start shaping. In this cycle, there's sometimes a provision for the further options of Basic Dough or Quick Dough.

Whole Wheat
Also known as the Whole Grain or Basic Wheat mode, it allows heavy whole grain flours to have a long kneading time and a rising time slightly longer than the Basic cycle rising time, producing a loaf that is lighter and higher. This works specifically well for all sorts of whole

wheat breads that contain more than 50 percent whole-grain flour. It is especially recommended for 100 percent whole-grain or whole wheat breads, and for breads that are made of specialty flours like barley or spelt. You can also have the choice of Basic or Quick setting within the cycle. On many of the newer models, their indicator alerts have been inbuilt such that it beeps to indicate when you should add any extra ingredients like raisins or nuts, during the cycle. Some of the models that have the preheat option at the beginning of their cycle usually preheat during the Whole Wheat cycle.

French Bread

A Crisp, European, or Homemade setting is usually available for the same purpose. This cycle is generally well-liked and well-received by users of bread machine baking. This setting is suitable for crusty country breads with zero sugar and fat because they require a longer length of time to rise and it also affords the yeast a long while to do its work. Older bread machines often have this cycle and it usually lasts for seven hours, which would be perfect for a traditional baker from France. It is also good for sourdough breads that contain yeast. The baking temperature of this cycle is about 325°F. The breads baked using this cycle are usually crisp with a soft inner crumb.

One Hour Cycle

The One Hour cycle is another type of shortened cycle that produces bread within one hour. The One Hour cycle eliminates more than one rise and is even more rapid that Quick Yeast Bread. Similar to the Quick Yeast Bread, the One Hour Cycle requires the use of instant or quick-rise yeast. Your owner's manual will provide information on how to regulate the yeast in a recipe for this cycle. I have personally noticed a decrease in taste and quality in breads made with this cycle, so I don't endorse using it. The One Hour cycle can be replaced with the Quick Yeast cycle when making gluten-free yeast breads.

Bake Only

In newer models of Bread Machine, a Bake Only cycle is sometimes programmed so that a dough prepared on the Dough cycle can be shaped into desired forms and then returned to the machine for baking. It can also be used for a cinnamon swirl bread, a hand-mixed dough, a commercial dough or in the event that you initially planned to bake your dough in the normal oven but changed your mind. When a cycle ends and your dough is not properly done, the Bake Only cycle is invaluable and you can program it to bake in increments for up to two hours. If you are doing different types of baking, this cycle works best.

Program

Certain machines have a function that allows a manual change of the cycle times to your preference, while being able to increase kneading, rising, or baking time as you need it. You can also program in the times for each of your recipes such that when you use a particular recipe, you don't need to program the time anymore, although this feature is only used by people who have become expert bakers and are proficient with the basic cycles.

Jam

Some newer machines have a feature where you can add small fresh fruit jams, with or without pectin and at the same time make fruit butters and chutneys. Make jam only in a machine designed for that purpose to prevent spills or leakage.

Delay Feature

This is a common and well-liked feature because you can program the machine at night and have fresh bread in the morning or meet fresh bread when you get home from work. There are some recipes that are not suitable for this cycle, such as recipes that include fresh ingredients like milk, cheese, eggs, fresh vegetables, and bacon, as they can become harmful at room temperature and turn sour or even result in food poisoning. Breads that require dry milk and powdered eggs are suitable for use with the Delay Timer. For optimum results while using the Delay Timer, make sure the yeast doesn't come in contact with the salt (because it would restrain its rising power) nor come in contact with any liquid (it would activate it before the mixing began) when the ingredients are together in the bread pan. Pour the liquid ingredients before any other, the salt should come after, then the dry ingredients, and the yeast should come at the end. Or switch the order around to suit your machine requirements. Many bread machine manuals insist this precaution for all recipes, but it is only needed when using the Delay Timer.

Preheat

Some bread machines have a Preheat or Rest period setting, which helps to keep ingredients put in the machine at uniform temperature by the time mixing starts just like how we used to warm flour on the oven door to encourage good rising and allow the yeast to perform at optimum capacity. This phase ranges from 15 to 30 minutes and the machine will be quiet during this phase since the blade is inactive. Some of the more complex machines allow you to ignore this feature but others don't. It is inbuilt in every baking cycle on some machines, while others like Breadman machines only have it on their Whole

Wheat cycle. Some people believe this feature produces better bread and like this feature, and some don't like it because it increases the time of the whole process.

Crust Control

This is a setting that gives you the option of a light, medium or dark crust in addition to being able to choose the cycle for your loaf. It does this by slightly altering the baking temperature or timing slightly. That way, you get to decide the finished look of your loaf. The crust setting also influences how well done a loaf is because it changes the baking time and temperature. For basic and whole-grain breads, I normally use the medium or normal crust setting, and I regularly check the loaf to make sure the bread is thoroughly baked.

If the crust on your bread comes out too light and the loaf is not properly baked, for another time, choose the dark crust setting and if the crust comes out too dark and the bread is overdone, choose light for the crust setting. Some people may like their whole wheat breads with light crust while some prefer dark crusts on their French breads but I normally set the crust on dark for my artisan and country breads, while light for sweetbreads, because they brown more quickly as a result of the higher sugar content. Note that certain ingredients in the loaf have a direct effect on how the crusts brown, so it's best to experiment with the crust setting.

Chapter 10 Differences of Sourdough bread and Quick bread without yeast

Sourdough - a natural agent for bread, traces of which date back to the Neolithic around 4000 BC - is a mixture of flour and water fermented by microorganisms and wild yeasts that are naturally contained in the flour and in the air. These microorganisms are also present in other raw materials such as apple juice or yogurt, which are sometimes used by bakers to give their sourdough a special aromatic note.

Sourdough – The Cameback

For bread preparation, there are various recipes, some of which have been unchanged for centuries. One thing is the same for all recipes: for them to succeed, they need a stimulant!

In addition to flour, salt, and water or any other liquid, it is essential for bread to succeed, a stimulant. While in recent decades, sourdough has increasingly been pushed into the background in favor of the less labor-consuming baker's yeast, it is currently experiencing a renaissance.

Sourdough care is complex and demanding. The knowledge related to its preparation was, therefore, almost forgotten with the introduction of baker's yeast. It caused the predominance of sourdough and its use to gradually decreased. This became especially true after the 1950s, when methods for inexpensive and efficient bread preparation have been developed. Nevertheless, sourdough in places like Switzerland is considered a cultural asset and is experiencing a true renaissance these days, as we've mentioned before. The taste and nutritional properties of sourdough baked goods are gaining in modern, health-conscious nutrition habits and diets - more and more bakers are returning to the traditional means of stimulation.

Sourdough - The Soul of a Bakery

A means of impulse or stimulation is therefore essential in the preparation of sourdough if the bread is to succeed. It is needed to "let the dough go", or, in other words, to loosen it, which is indispensable if the bread is to become wholesome. If dough does not ferment, or if it does so for too short an amount of time (1 to 2 hours), phytic acid will not degrade and will inhibit the absorption of minerals in the metabolism. It will not rise and will be little to no digestible.

Since the sourcing of sourdough is influenced by the choice of liquid for preparation, no sourdough is like the other. This is because water quality and hardness, which differ from source to source, will influence the microflora. For its complexity, sourdough is not without reason the pride of a baker and the heart of a bakery.

Sourdough - Aromatic and Healthy

The return of sourdough has to do with the return of regional products and healthy nutrition. Sourdough owes its qualities to lactic acid bacteria and yeast fungi, which provide the fermentation process. The resulting carbon dioxide not only loosens the dough but also improves the aroma, taste, and shelf life of the bread.

Long-handled sourdough makes the bread wholesome. The longer a dough is led, the more starch can be broken down by the naturally occurring enzymes. Starch, in turn, is responsible for the water binding in the dough. The more starch there is, the more water is bound. The result: The bread is dry and crumbly, does not taste, and is less well digestible.

Of particular importance is sourdough in the use of rye flour. Unlike wheat flour, where pure baker's yeast can be used as a leavening agent, rye requires the addition of acid so that the bread does not remain flat. The lactic acid bacteria of sourdough produce these in the form of lactic acid and acetic acid. The lactic acid bacteria strengthen the flavors and make the pastry elastic.

The use of sourdough is also geographically different. While rye or wheat flour is used for sourdough-baked Swiss bread, German and Austrian bakers use almost exclusively rye flour. The further south one comes, the less rye grows. Rye flour is then replaced by the lighter wheat flour, and so, for example, the classic French baguette is traditionally baked with wheat sourdough.

Sourdough is a leavening agent prepared with active or reactivatable microorganisms (mainly lactic acid bacteria and yeasts), which continuously forms acids upon the addition of cereal products and water. This produces lactic acid-forming (homofermentative) and acetic acid-forming (heterofermentative) lactic acid bacteria as well as yeasts. The heterofermentative bacteria produce small amounts of carbon dioxide, which, together with the carbon dioxide of the alcoholic yeast fermentation forms fermentation gas and provides the impulse without which bread can not succeed. As an alternative to sourdough, yeast can be used as a leavening agent. The recovery of a drivable sourdough Anstellguts lasts at least a week - the longer the sourdough is led, the tastier and wholesome is the baked bread.

The term "sourdough guide" describes time, temperature, and ingredient ratios in the production of the dough. The Anstellgut is a remainder sourdough, which is stored for later use. Anstellgut either can be removed from each set for the baking day sourdough or separately managed and refreshed. The crop should be mixed every 7 to 10 days at the latest with equal parts of flour and water and so refreshed.

Once sourced, sourdough can be used as a base to infinity. For this reason, it only has to be "fed" regularly - every one to two weeks - with flour and liquid. The liquid used is usually water, as the ground flora already exists.

Phytic acid is a substance that is found in cereals, especially in the outer layers and in the seedling, and, with minerals, enters into a poorly soluble compound. This complicates or blocks the absorption of important minerals such as calcium, magnesium, zinc, and iron in the human body. In fact, nature does provide an enzyme called phytase, which prevents phytic acid from binding valuable minerals. This enzyme sits exactly where most of the phytic acid is found: in the germ and in the bran.

Phytase is activated only by long sourdough guidance and by soaking fresh grain porridge. Even natural vitamin C in fresh fruit (apples, berries, citrus fruits) has the ability to deactivate the phytic acid and lay the foundation for an edible and wholesome end product.

Quick Bread

Also known as Cake, this setting is good for batters without yeast, leavened with baking soda or baking powder, e.g. quick breads and loaf cakes. This cycle mixes the ingredients and bakes with zero rise time. Older models require the mixing to be done by hand while the batter is poured into the pan, without installing the kneading blade. There is also an option for extended baking at intervals of one minute. This cycle works well with packaged mixes for quick bread, cornbread, and pound cake. The setting is usually automatic on some models but on others, it has to be programmed manually.

Quick Yeast Bread

The older models of bread machines have this cycle programmed separately, while the newer models have it as an option within the Basic, Dough and Whole Wheat cycles. This program is specifically designed to be used with instant or quick rise yeast and is also known by other names like Quick Bake, Turbo or just Quick. It skips the second rise and shortens the total cycle time by forty-five minutes to one hour. See your owner's manual to know how to adjust the yeast. The ingredients must be at room temperature before putting them in the machine during this cycle. Since the action time of the yeast has already been shortened

having the ingredients at room temperature before adding to the mix ensures that the yeast will immediately get activated. This cycle can be used instead of the One Hour cycle for gluten-free yeast breads since these doughs need a short rising time. Be informed that this cycle is different from the Quick Bread cycle. Even though shortened, this cycle still produces a nice loaf of bread.

Chapter 11 Breakfast

Cheese Bread

Preparation Time: 30 minutes
Cooking Time: 2 hours
Servings: 5
Ingredients:
2 ¾ cups (500 g) wheat flour
1 teaspoon dry yeast
1 ½ teaspoons salt
2 teaspoons sugar
3 tablespoons soft butter
¾ cup (200 ml) warm water
1 cup (150 g) hard cheese
Spicy herbs to taste (dill,
rosemary, thyme, etc.)
Directions:
The flour needs to be sifted.
If the instructions for the
bread maker say to add dry
foods first, then do so.
Grate cheese on a large grater.
Put aside a small part, about a
quarter. Most of the cheese is
sent to flour and roll in it.
Add
all the other ingredients.
Whisk the yolk.
Ten minutes before the end of
baking, open the bread maker

and grease the loaf with the
whipped yolk
sprinkle the remaining cheese
on top.
Our cheesy bread is ready! It
smells delicious, and tastes
yummy! Enjoy!
Nutrition: Calories 648
Total Fat 41.3g
Saturated Fat 25.5g
Cholesterol 86gSodium 862mg
Total Carbohydrate 54.7g
Dietary Fiber 2g
Total Sugars 1.9g
Protein 14.7g

Vanilla Milk Bread

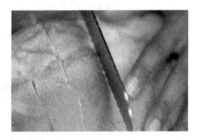

Preparation Time: 30-45
minutes
Cooking Time: 2 hours
Servings: 8
Ingredients:
4 ½ cups (580 g) wheat flour
1 ¾ cups (370 ml = 12 ½ oz)
milk
1 tablespoon sugar
1 packet vanilla sugar
2 tablespoons olive oil
2 teaspoons dried yeast
2 teaspoons salt
Directions:

Pour milk into the form, along with 3 ½ ounces of water and olive oil.
Put in the flour. Then put sugar, vanilla sugar, and salt in different corners of the form. Make a groove in the flour, and put in the yeast.
Bake on the Basic program. Cool the bread and enjoy.
Nutrition: Calories 328
Total Fat 5.7g
Saturated Fat 1.4g
Cholesterol 4g Sodium 610mg
Total Carbohydrate 59.1g
Dietary Fiber 2.1g
Total Sugars 4.6g Protein 9.4g

Traditional English Bread

Preparation Time: 30-45 minutes
Cooking Time: 2 hours
Servings: 8
Ingredients:
4 ½ cups (600 g) wheat flour
½ cup (80 g) polenta
5 tablespoons (90 g) molasses
2 teaspoons lemon juice
3 tablespoons butter
2 teaspoons dried yeast
2 ½ teaspoons salt

Directions: Pour 16 ¼ oz (480 ml) of water, molasses, and lemon juice into the mold.
Add flour and polenta put salt and butter in at different corners of the mold. Make a groove in the flour, and then add the yeast. Bake on the BASIC program. Cool the bread.
Nutrition: Calories 368
Total Fat 5.2g, Saturated Fat 2.9g, Protein 8.4g
Cholesterol 11g
Sodium 767mg
Total Carbohydrate 71g
Dietary Fiber 2.4g
Total Sugars 7.3g

Oatmeal Zucchini Bread

Preparation Time: 10 minutes
Cooking Time: 20-30 minutes
Servings: Makes 1 loaf
Ingredients:
8 SLICES / 1 POUND
⅓ cup milk, at 80°F to 90°F
½ cup finely shredded zucchini
¼ teaspoon freshly squeezed lemon juice, at room temperature

2 teaspoons olive oil
2 teaspoons sugar
⅔ teaspoon salt
½ cup quick oats
½ cup whole-wheat flour
1 cup white bread flour
1½ teaspoons bread machine
or instant yeast
12 SLICES / 1½ POUNDS
½ cup milk, at 80°F to 90°F
¾ cup finely shredded
zucchini
¼ teaspoon freshly squeezed
lemon juice, at room
temperature
1 tablespoon olive oil
1 tablespoon sugar
1 teaspoon salt
¾ cup quick oats
¾ cup whole-wheat flour
1½ cups white bread flour
2¼ teaspoons bread machine
or instant yeast
16 SLICES / 2 POUNDS
⅔ cup milk, at 80°F to 90°F
1 cup finely shredded zucchini
⅓ teaspoon freshly squeezed
lemon juice, at room
temperature
4 teaspoons olive oil
4 teaspoons sugar
1⅓ teaspoons salt
1 cup quick oats
1 cup whole-wheat flour
2 cups white bread flour
2¼ teaspoons bread machine
or instant yeast
Directions:
Place the ingredients in your
bread machine as
recommended by the
manufacturer.

Program the machine for
Basic/White bread, select light
or medium crust, and press
Start.
When the loaf is done, remove
the bucket from the machine.
Let the loaf cool for 5
minutes.
Gently shake the bucket to
remove the loaf, and turn it
out onto a rack to cool.
Nutrition: Calories: 127
Total Fat: 2g
Saturated Fat: 0g
Carbohydrates: 23g
fiber: 1g
Sodium: 200mg
Protein: 4g

Moist Oatmeal Apple Bread

Preparation Time: 10 minutes
Cooking Time: 20-30 minutes
Servings: Makes 1 loaf
Ingredients:
8 SLICES / 1 POUND
½ cup milk, at 80°F to 90°F
2¾ tablespoons unsweetened
applesauce, at room
temperature
2 teaspoons melted butter,
cooled
2 teaspoons sugar
⅔ teaspoon salt
¼ teaspoon ground cinnamon
Pinch ground nutmeg
2¾ tablespoons quick oats
1½ cups white bread flour
1½ teaspoons bread machine
or active dry yeast
12 SLICES / 1½ POUNDS
⅔ cup milk, at 80°F to 90°F

¼ cup unsweetened
applesauce, at room
temperature
1 tablespoon melted butter,
cooled
1 tablespoon sugar
1 teaspoon salt
½ teaspoon ground cinnamon
Pinch ground nutmeg
¼ cup quick oats
2¼ cups white bread flour
2¼ teaspoons bread machine
or active dry yeast
16 SLICES / 2 POUNDS
1 cup milk, at 80°F to 90°F
⅓ cup unsweetened
applesauce, at room
temperature
4 teaspoons melted butter,
cooled
4 teaspoons sugar
1⅓ teaspoons salt
¾ teaspoon ground cinnamon
Pinch ground nutmeg
⅓ cup quick oats
3 cups white bread flour
2¼ teaspoons bread machine
or active dry yeast

Directions:
Place the ingredients in your
bread machine as
recommended by the
manufacturer.
Program the machine for
Basic/White bread, select light
or medium crust, and press
Start.
When the loaf is done, remove
the bucket from the machine.
Let the loaf cool for 5
minutes.

Gently shake the bucket to
remove the loaf, and turn it
out onto a rack to cool.
Nutrition:
Calories: 115
Total Fat: 2g
Saturated Fat: 1g
Carbohydrates: 22g
fiber: 1g
Sodium: 208mg
Protein: 3g

Hearty Oatmeal Loaf
Preparation Time: 30-45
minutes
Cooking Time: 30-45 minutes
Servings: Makes 1 loaf
Ingredients:
¾ cup water at 80 degrees F
2 tablespoons melted butter,
cooled
2 tablespoons sugar
1 teaspoon salt
¾ cup quick oats
1½ cups white bread flour
1 teaspoon instant yeast
Directions:
Add all of the ingredients to
your bread machine, carefully
following the instructions of
the manufacturer.
Set the program of your bread
machine to Basic/White Bread
and set crust type to Medium.
Press START.
Wait until the cycle completes.
Once the loaf is ready, take the
bucket out and let the loaf
cool for 5 minutes.
Gently shake the bucket to
remove the loaf.
Transfer to a cooling rack,
slice, and serve.

Nutrition: Total Carbs: 26g,
Fiber: 1g
protein: 4g
fat: 4g,
Calories: 149

Pecan Apple Spice Bread

Preparation Time: 30-45 minutes
Cooking Time: 30-45 minutes
Servings: Makes 1 loaf

Ingredients:
16 slice bread (2 pounds)
½ cup lukewarm water
3 tablespoons canola oil
1 teaspoon apple cider vinegar
3 tablespoons light brown sugar, packed
1 cup Granny Smith apples, grated
3 eggs, room temperature, slightly beaten
¾ cup brown rice flour
¾ cup tapioca flour
¾ cup millet flour
½ cup corn starch
2 tablespoons apple pie spice
1 tablespoon xanthan gum
1 teaspoon table salt
2 teaspoons bread machine yeast
½ cup pecans, chopped
12 slice bread (1½ pounds)
⅓ cup lukewarm water
2¼ tablespoons canola oil
¾ teaspoon apple cider vinegar
2¼ tablespoons light brown sugar, packed
¾ cup Granny Smith apples, grated
2 eggs, room temperature, slightly beaten
½ cup brown rice flour
½ cup tapioca flour
½ cup millet flour
⅓ cup corn starch
1½ tablespoons apple pie spice
¾ tablespoon xanthan gum
¾ teaspoon table salt
1¼ teaspoons bread machine yeast
⅓ cup pecans, chopped

Directions:
Choose the size of loaf you would like to make and measure your ingredients. Add all of the ingredients except for the pecans to the bread pan in the order listed above. Place the pan in the bread machine and close the lid.
Turn on the bread maker. Select the White/Basic or Gluten-Free (if your machine has this setting) setting, then the loaf size, and finally the crust color. Start the cycle. When the machine signals to add ingredients, add the chopped pecans. When the cycle is finished and the bread is baked, carefully remove the pan from the machine. Use a pot holder as the handle will be very hot. Let rest for a few minutes.
Remove the bread from the pan and allow to cool on a wire rack for at least 10 minutes before slicing.
Nutrition: Calories 154 fat 5 g carbs 22.3 g sodium174 mg protein 3.1 g

Pumpkin Jalapeno Bread

Preparation Time: 30-45 minutes
Cooking Time: 30-45 minutes
Servings: Makes 1 loaf

Ingredients:

16 slice bread (2 pounds)
¾ cup lukewarm water
2 large eggs, beaten
½ cup pumpkin puree
3 tablespoons honey
2½ tablespoons vegetable oil
1 teaspoon apple cider vinegar
2 teaspoons sugar
1 teaspoon table salt
¾ cup brown rice flour
¾ cup tapioca flour
½ cup corn starch
½ cup yellow corn meal
1 tablespoon xanthan gum
1 medium jalapeno pepper, seeded and deveined
2 teaspoons crushed red pepper flakes
2 teaspoons bread machine yeast
12 slice bread (1½ pounds)
½ cup lukewarm water
2 medium eggs, beaten
⅓ cup pumpkin puree
2¼ tablespoons honey
1½ tablespoons vegetable oil
¾ teaspoon apple cider vinegar
1½ teaspoons sugar
¾ teaspoon table salt
½ cup brown rice flour
½ cup tapioca flour
⅓ cup corn starch
⅓ cup yellow corn meal
¾ tablespoon xanthan gum

1 small jalapeno pepper, seeded and deveined
1½ teaspoons crushed red pepper flakes
1¼ teaspoons bread machine yeast

Directions:

Choose the size of loaf you would like to make and measure your ingredients. Add the ingredients to the bread pan in the order listed above.
Place the pan in the bread machine and close the lid. Turn on the bread maker. Select the White/Basic or Gluten-Free (if your machine has this setting) setting, then the loaf size, and finally the crust color. Start the cycle. When the cycle is finished and the bread is baked, carefully remove the pan from the machine. Use a pot holder as the handle will be very hot. Let rest for a few minutes.
Remove the bread from the pan and allow to cool on a wire rack for at least 10 minutes before slicing.

Nutrition:
Calories 124
fat 2.3 g
carbs 21.7 g
sodium179 mg
protein 2 g

Walnut Banana Bread

Preparation Time: 30-45 minutes
Cooking Time: 30-45 minutes
Servings: Makes 1 loaf
Ingredients:
16 slice bread (2 pounds)
½ cup lukewarm water
3 tablespoons canola oil
1 teaspoon apple cider vinegar
2 eggs, beaten
2 small banana, mashed
1 teaspoon table salt
¾ cup brown rice flour
¾ cup white rice flour
¾ cup amaranth flour
½ cup corn starch
1 tablespoon xanthan gum
1 teaspoon cinnamon
½ teaspoon nutmeg
2 teaspoons bread machine yeast
1 cup walnuts, chopped
12 slice bread (1½ pounds)
⅓ cup lukewarm water
2 tablespoons canola oil
¾ teaspoon apple cider vinegar
2 eggs, beaten
1½ small bananas, mashed
¾ teaspoon table salt
½ cup brown rice flour
½ cup white rice flour
½ cup amaranth flour
⅓ cup corn starch
¾ tablespoon xanthan gum
¾ teaspoon cinnamon
⅓ teaspoon nutmeg
1½ teaspoons bread machine yeast
¾ cup walnuts, chopped
Directions:

Choose the size of loaf you would like to make and measure your ingredients. Add the ingredients to the bread pan in the order listed above.
Place the pan in the bread machine and close the lid. Turn on the bread maker. Select the Quick/Rapid setting, then the loaf size, and finally the crust color. Start the cycle.
When the cycle is finished and the bread is baked, carefully remove the pan from the machine. Use a pot holder as the handle will be very hot. Let rest for a few minutes.
Remove the bread from the pan and allow to cool on a wire rack for at least 10 minutes before slicing.
Nutrition:
Calories 193
fat 8.3 g
carbs 24.4 g
sodium172 mg
protein 4.2 g

Banana Bread

Preparation Time: 30 minutes
Cooking Time: 3 hours
Servings: Makes 1 loaf
Ingredients:
2 cups wheat flour, sifted
¾ cup brown sugar
2 soft bananas, mashed
3 tablespoons butter, melted
1 teaspoon active dry yeast
2 whole eggs, slightly beaten
½ teaspoon vanilla sugar
½ teaspoon ground cinnamon

15 walnuts, crushed
Directions:
Prepare all of the ingredients
for your bread and measuring
means (a cup, a spoon, kitchen
scales).
Carefully measure the
ingredients into the pan.
Place all of the ingredients,
into the bread bucket in the
right order, following the
manual for your bread
machine.
Close the cover.
Select the program of your
bread machine to SWEET
BREAD and choose the crust
color to MEDIUM.
Press START.
Wait until the program
completes.
When done, take the bucket
out and let it cool for 5-10
minutes.
Shake the loaf from the pan
and let cool for 30 minutes on
a cooling rack.
Slice, serve and enjoy the taste
of fragrant homemade bread.
Nutrition:
Calories 373
Total Fat 9.3g
Saturated Fat 4.3g
Cholesterol 70mg
Sodium 63mg
Total Carbohydrate 67.2g
Dietary Fiber 2.8g
Total Sugars 30.1g
Protein 7.3g

Lemon Fruit Bread
Preparation Time: 30 minutes
Cooking Time: 3 hours

Servings: Makes 1 loaf
Ingredients:
1 whole egg
1 cup (250 ml, 8 oz) lukewarm
milk (80 degrees F)
¼ cup (60 g, 2 oz) butter,
melted and cooled
1/3 cup (80 g) white sugar
4 cups (500 g, 18 oz) wheat
flour
1 tablespoon active dry yeast
1 teaspoon salt
½ cup (100 g) candied lemons
1½ teaspoon lemon zest,
grated
½ cup (50 g) raisins
½ cup (50 g) cashew nuts,
chopped
Directions:
Prepare all of the ingredients
for your bread and measuring
means (a cup, a spoon, kitchen
scales).
Carefully measure the
ingredients into the pan,
except the raisins, zest, lemons,
and nuts.
Place all of the ingredients,
into the bread bucket in the
right order, following the
manual for your bread
machine.
Close the cover.
Select the program of your
bread machine to BASIC and
choose the crust color to
MEDIUM.
Press START.
After the signal, add the
raisins, zest, lemons, and nuts
to the dough.
Wait until the program
completes.

When done, take the bucket out and let it cool for 5-10 minutes.
Shake the loaf from the pan and let cool for 30 minutes on a cooling rack.
Slice, serve and enjoy the taste of fragrant homemade bread.
Nutrition:
Calories 438, Total Fat 10.6 g, Saturated Fat 4.9 g, Cholesterol 38 mg sodium358 mg, Total Carbohydrate 76.7 g, Dietary Fiber 2.5 g
Total Sugars 23.1 g
protein 10 g, Vitamin D 6 mcg, Calcium 60 mg, Iron 4 mg, Potassium 211 mg

Coconut Milk Bread

Preparation Time: 30 minutes
Cooking Time: 3 hours
Servings: Makes 1 loaf

Ingredients:

1 whole egg
½ cup (100 ml, 4 oz) lukewarm milk (80 degrees F)
½ cup (120 ml, 4 oz) lukewarm coconut milk (80 degrees F)
¼ cup (50 g, 2 oz) butter, melted and cooled
2 tablespoons (50 g) liquid honey
4 cups (500 g, 18 oz) wheat flour, sifted
1 tablespoon active dry yeast
1 teaspoon salt
½ cup (100 g, 6 oz) coconut chips

Directions:

Prepare all of the ingredients for your bread and measuring means (a cup, a spoon, kitchen scales).

Carefully measure the ingredients into the pan, except the coconut chips.

Place all of the ingredients, into the bread bucket in the right order, following the manual for your bread machine.

Close the cover.

Select the program of your bread machine to SWEET and choose the crust color to MEDIUM.

Press START.

After the signal, add the coconut chips into the dough. Wait until the program completes.

When done, take the bucket out and let it cool for 5-10 minutes.

Shake the loaf from the pan and let cool for 30 minutes on a cooling rack.

Slice, serve and enjoy the taste of fragrant homemade bread.

Nutrition:

Calories 421, Total Fat 15.3 g, Saturated Fat 11.7 g, Cholesterol 37 mg sodium350 mg, Total Carbohydrate 61.9 g, Dietary Fiber 3.2 g

Total Sugars 11.7 g protein 9.5 g, Vitamin D 6 mcg, Calcium 33 mg, Iron 4 mg, Potassium 157 mg

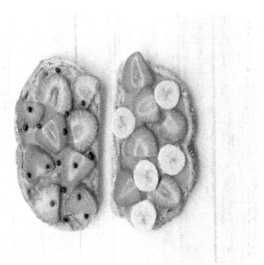

Egg Bread

Preparation Time: 30-45 minutes
Cooking Time: 30-45 minutes
Servings: Makes 1 loaf
Ingredients:
4 cups (520 g) bread flour, sifted
1 cup (230 ml) lukewarm milk
2 whole eggs
1 teaspoon active dry yeast
1 ½ teaspoons salt
2 ¼ tablespoons white sugar
1 ½ tablespoons butter, melted
Directions:
Prepare all of the ingredients for your bread and measuring means (a cup, a spoon, kitchen scales).
Carefully measure the ingredients into the pan.
Place all of the ingredients into the bread bucket in the right order, following the manual for your bread machine.
Close the cover.
Select the program of your bread machine to BASIC and choose the crust color to MEDIUM.
Press START.
Wait until the program completes.
When done, take the bucket out and let it cool for 5-10 minutes.
Shake the loaf from the pan and let cool for 30 minutes on a cooling rack.
Slice, serve and enjoy the taste of fragrant homemade bread.
Nutrition:

Calories 319
Total Fat 5.6g
Saturated Fat 2.7g
Cholesterol 56g
Sodium 495mg
Total Carbohydrate 56.7g
Dietary Fiber 1.8g
Total Sugars 6.5g
Protein 9.6g

Egg Liqueur Bread

Preparation Time: 30 minutes
Cooking Time: 2 hours 10 minutes
Servings: Makes 1 loaf
Ingredients:
3 whole eggs
½ cup (100 ml) egg liqueur
½ cup (100 g, 4 oz) butter, melted
½ cup (120 g, 4 oz) brown sugar
1 tablespoon vanilla sugar
2 ½ cups (300 g, 11.25 oz) wheat flour
1 tablespoon baking powder
Directions:
Prepare all of the ingredients for your bread and measuring means (a cup, a spoon, kitchen scales).
Carefully measure the ingredients into the pan.
Place all of the ingredients, into the bread bucket in the right order, following the manual for your bread machine.
Close the cover.
Select the program of your bread machine to CAKE and choose the crust color to LIGHT.

Press START.
Wait until the program completes.
When done, take the bucket out and let it cool for 5-10 minutes.
Shake the loaf from the pan and let cool for 30 minutes on a cooling rack.
Slice, serve and enjoy the taste of fragrant homemade bread.
Nutrition:
Calories 349, Total Fat 14.3 g, Saturated Fat 7.9 g, Cholesterol 92 mg sodium107 mg, Total Carbohydrate 46.8 g, Dietary Fiber 1.1 g
Total Sugars 12.8 g
protein 6.7 g, Vitamin D 14 mcg, Calcium 99 mg, Iron 2 mg, Potassium 257 mg

Chocolate Date Sesame Bread

Preparation Time: 1 hour 30 minutes
Cooking Time: 1 hour 30 minutes
Servings: 12
Ingredients:
½ cup butter, softened
1 ½ teaspoons salt
3 tablespoons sugar
¾ cup milk
¾ cup water
4 cups flour
½ cup chocolate
2 tablespoons cocoa powder
3 tablespoons sesame seeds
½ cup dates, pitted
1 tablespoon fresh yeast
Directions:

Sift the flour. Cut the dates finely. Rub the chocolate on a fine grater.
Combine the cocoa and water, and stir well so that there are no lumps. Add the milk and stir again.
Put the softened butter in the bread container. Then add salt, sugar, the mixture of cocoa and milk, chocolate, and sesame. Then put in the flour and yeast.
Roll dates in flour
Turn on the bread maker.
After finishing, take out the bread container and take out the hot bread. Cool it for 1 hour on a grate, covered with a towel.
Nutrition:
Calories 315
Total Fat 11.8g
Saturated Fat 6.8g
Cholesterol 23
Sodium 360mg
Total Carbohydrate 46.7g
Dietary Fiber 2.7g
Total Sugars 12.7g
Protein 6.5g

Sweet Yogurt Cherry Bread

Preparation Time: 1 hour 30 minutes
Cooking Time: 1 hour 30 minutes
Servings: 8
Ingredients:
½ cup warm water
½ cup fruit yogurt
2 ½ tablespoons sugar
2 cups flour

1 ½ teaspoons yeast
½ cup dried cherries
Directions:
Put the ingredients in the bread maker in the manner indicated in your instructions. Enable the program.
After it finishes, take out the bread and cool it on a grate.
Nutrition:
Calories 198
Total Fat 0.8g
Saturated Fat 0.3g
Cholesterol 1
Sodium 13mg
Total Carbohydrate 42.2g
Dietary Fiber 1.6g
Total Sugars 9.4g
Protein 5.5g

Chocolate Bread

Preparation Time: 1 hour 30 minutes
Cooking Time: 1 hour 30 minutes
Servings: 8
Ingredients:
1 cup water
2 1/3 cups wholemeal flour
½ cup wheat flour
½ cup rice flour
¾ cup dark chocolate
½ cup sour cream
1 tablespoon butter
1 ½ tablespoons cocoa
1 tablespoon sugar
1 teaspoon yeast
1 teaspoon salt
Directions:
In the bowl of the bread maker, pour in water and add sour cream.

Top with flour. In the corners of the bowl, pour cocoa powder, yeast, sugar, and salt so that they do not come in contact.
Turn on the Knead program. When the dough turns into a ball, press PAUSE and add the butter. Continue the kneading dough.
Put the dough into a bowl and put in a warm place for 1 hour.
The dough should increase 2-3 times.
Transfer the dough to the table, lightly pouring the surface of the table with flour. Cut the chocolate into small pieces. Roll the dough into an oval-shaped formation. Top with the pieces of chocolate. Roll the dough into a roll.
Transfer the dough to the bread maker and leave it for 1 hour.
Bake bread in bread maker in the Baking mode for 30 minutes.
Serve chocolate bread with tea, milk, or coffee. Chocolate bread is suitable for making dessert sandwiches and perfectly matches with condensed milk, nut butter, and confiture.
BON APPETIT!
Nutrition:
Calories 183
Total Fat 8.1g
Saturated Fat 4.8g
Cholesterol 10
Sodium 310mg
Total Carbohydrate 25.3g

Dietary Fiber 1.5g
Total Sugars 8.8g
Protein 2.6g

Raisin Cake

Preparation Time: 1 hour 30 minutes
Cooking Time: 1 hour 30 minutes
Servings: 8
Ingredients:
2 eggs
¾ cup butter
1/3 cup milk
1 teaspoon salt
4 tablespoons sugar
2 ¾ cups flour
2 teaspoons dry yeast
¾ cup raisins
Directions:
Scald raisins with boiling water, drain, and dry.
Cut butter into slices.
In the bowl of the bread maker, beat the eggs, pour in the milk, and add the butter.
Add salt and sugar.
Sift the flour.
Put it in a container.
Add the dry yeast.
Set the bread maker in the desired mode, selecting the weight of the cake and the color of the crust. Add the raisins after the signal.
Remove cake carefully, so as not to burn your hands. Move to a grate and leave until completely cooled. Cover with icing or sprinkle with powdered sugar.
Store the cake in a plastic bag in a cool place.
BON APPETIT!
Nutrition:
Calories 396
Total Fat 19.1g
Saturated Fat 11.5g
Cholesterol 88
Sodium 436mg
Total Carbohydrate 50.5g
Dietary Fiber 1.9g
Total Sugars 14.7g
Protein 7.1g

Delicious Cake For Tea

Preparation Time: 1 hour 45 minutes
Cooking Time: 1 hour 45 minutes
Servings: 8
Ingredients:
2 ½ teaspoons yeast
3 ½ cups flour
½ teaspoon salt
6 tablespoons sugar
1 bag vanillin
6 tablespoons oil
3 eggs
1 cup water
1 cup peeled and diced apples
You can also add nuts or raisins
Directions:
Place all the ingredients in the bread maker in the order given in the instructions.
In the process of baking, the bread will rise quite a bit.
After cooking, take out the bread and cool on a grate.
Nutrition:
Calories 379
Total Fat 12.5g
Saturated Fat 1.9g
Cholesterol 61
Sodium 173mg
Total Carbohydrate 59.1g
Dietary Fiber 3.1g

Total Sugars 15.1g
Protein 8.4g

Brioche

Preparation Time: 1 hour 45 minutes
Cooking Time: 1 hour 45 minutes
Servings: 8
Ingredients: 1/3 cup warm milk
2 tablespoons sugar
1 ½ teaspoon active dry yeast
2 large eggs 1 teaspoon salt
2 ½ cups bread flour
½ cup butter, melted
Directions: Put ingredients in the bread maker according to the instructions - first liquid products, then dry, and then dry yeast at the top. When the bread is ready, remove it from the bread maker and cut into portions. Serve with butter or marmalade jam.
Nutrition: Calories 147
Total Fat 13g
Saturated Fat 7.8g
Cholesterol 78mg
Sodium 395mg
Total Carbohydrate 5.8g
Dietary Fiber 0.2g
Total Sugars 3.6g Protein 2.6g

Lemon Cake

Preparation Time: 1 hour 30 minutes
Cooking Time: 1 hour 30 minutes
Servings: 8
Ingredients:
3 eggs
½ cup butter
½ teaspoon salt
4/5 cup sugar
2 ½ cups flour
2 ½ teaspoons baking powder
juice and peel of one small lemon
Directions:
Combine the eggs, sugar, and salt.
Beat with a mixer into a thick foam.
Wash the lemon carefully.
With a small grater, peel the lemon peel and then squeeze the juice.
In the bowl of the bread maker, pour in the eggs with sugar foam. Add softened butter, lemon zest, and juice.
Mix flour with baking powder.
Pour the flour into the bowl of the bread maker.
Set to the desired mode, Dough, for 30 minutes, then Bake for the 2 hours.
Turn the cooked cake onto a grate and cool. Sprinkle with powdered sugar.
Serve, and enjoy.
Nutrition:
Calories 346
Total Fat 13.6g
Saturated Fat 7.9g
Cholesterol 92mg
Sodium 254mg
Total Carbohydrate 51.2g
Dietary Fiber 1.1g
Total Sugars 21g
Protein 6.3g

Raisin Bread

Preparation Time: 5 minutes
Cooking Time: 3 h 5 minutes

Serving: 15
Ingredients:
1 C. milk
3 tbsp butter, softened
3 C. bread flour
3 tbsp honey
2 1/4 tsp bread machine yeast
1 tbsp brown sugar
1 C. raisins
1 egg
1 tsp salt
1 tsp ground cinnamon
Directions:
In a bread machine pan, place all the ingredients except raisins in order as suggested by the manual.
Select the Sweet Dough cycle and press the Start button.
After the beef sounds add the raisins in the bread machine pan.
Nutrition:
Calories 175 kcal
Fat 3.5 g
Carbohydrates 31.7g
Protein 4.7 g
Cholesterol 20 mg
Sodium 185 mg

Sweet Raisin Bread
Preparation Time: 15 minutes
Total Time: 3 h 15 minutes
Servings: 12
Ingredients:
1 1/2 C. water
1 tbsp brown sugar
2 tbsp cider vinegar
3 tbsp unsweetened cocoa powder
2 1/2 C. bread flour
1 tsp instant coffee granules
1 C. rye flour

1 tbsp caraway seed
1 tsp salt
1/4 tsp fennel seed
2 tbsp margarine
2 tsp active dry yeast
2 tbsp dark corn syrup
Directions:
In a bread machine pan, add all the ingredients in order as suggested by the manual.
Select the Whole Wheat with Regular Crust cycle and press the Start button.
After the completion of cycle, place the bread onto a wire rack to cool for at least 1 hour before slicing.
Cut into desired sized slices and enjoy.
Nutrition: Calories 172 kcal
Fat 2.7 g Carbohydrates 32.6g
Protein 4.8 g Cholesterol 0 mg
Sodium 222 mg

Rye Bread
Preparation Time: 25 minutes
Total Time: 2 h 28 minutes
Servings: 12
Ingredients:
1 1/8 C. water
1 tbsp unsweetened cocoa powder
2 tbsp molasses
3/4 tsp caraway seed
1 tbsp vegetable oil
2 tsp bread machine yeast
1 tsp salt
2 C. all-purpose flour
1 1/2 C. rye flour
3 tbsp packed brown sugar
Directions:

In a bread machine pan, add
all the ingredients in order as
suggested by the manual.
Select the Basic cycle and press
the Start button.
Nutrition:
Calories 159 kcal Fat 1.6 g
Carbohydrates 32.5g
Protein 3.6 g Cholesterol 0 mg
Sodium 197 mg

Simple Bread Toscana

Preparation Time: 5 minutes
Total Time: 3 hours
Servings: 12
Ingredients:
1 1/2 C. water
3 1/2 C. bread flour
1 tbsp white sugar
2 1/2 tsp active dry yeast
1 1/2 tsp salt
Directions:
In a bread machine pan, add
all the ingredients in order as
suggested by the manual.
Select the Light or Medium
Crust cycle and press the Start
button.
Nutrition:
Calories 151 kcal
Fat 0.7 g
Carbohydrates 30.3g
Protein 5.1 g
Cholesterol 0 mg
Sodium 292 mg

Minced Cheddar Bread

Preparation Time: 5 minutes
Total Time: 3 hours 5 minutes
Servings: 12
Ingredients:
1 1/8 C. warm water
3 C. bread flour
2 tsp garlic powder
2 tbsp dry milk powder
3 tbsp dried minced onion
2 tbsp white sugar
1 C. shredded sharp Cheddar cheese
1 1/2 tsp salt
2 tbsp margarine
2 tsp active dry yeast

Directions:
In a bread machine pan, add the water, flour, powdered milk, sugar, salt, margarine and yeast in order as suggested by the manual.
Select the Basic cycle with the Light Crust and press the Start button.
After the beep sounds in the pan, add the shredded cheese, 2 tbsp of the onion flakes and garlic powder.
After the completion of cycle, sprinkle the bread with the remaining onion flakes.
Nutrition: Calories 205 kcal Fat 6.2 g Carbohydrates 29.1g Protein 7.8 g Cholesterol 12 mg
Sodium 391 mg

Tarragon and Parmesan

Preparation Time: 45 minutes

Total Time: 1 hour 15 minutes
Servings: 10
Ingredients:
1 egg, beaten
1/4 C. butter, melted
2 tbsp butter, softened
1 tsp paprika
1/2 C. water
1/4 C. grated Parmesan cheese
1/2 C. milk
1/2 tsp garlic powder
1 tsp salt
1 tsp dried minced onion
1 tbsp white sugar
1/2 tsp rubbed sage
2 1/2 C. bread flour
1/2 tsp dried tarragon
1 (.25 oz.) package active dry yeast

Directions:
In a bread machine pan, add the egg, 2 tbsp of the butter, water, milk, salt, sugar, bread flour and yeast in order as suggested by the manual.
Select the Dough cycle and press the Start button.
After the completion of cycle, place the dough onto a lightly floured surface.
In shallow bowl, add the melted butter.
Add the cheese, tarragon, sage, onion flakes, garlic powder and paprika in another shallow bowl and mix well.
Divide the dough into 20-25 equal sized portions.
Coat dough portions with the butter and ten with the cheese mixture evenly.
In the bottom of a lightly greased Bundt pan, arrange the dough portions.

With a damp kitchen towel, cover the Bundt pan and keep aside in warm area for at least 30-35 minutes.
Meanwhile, set your oven to 350 degrees F.
Place in the oven for about 30-35 minutes.
Enjoy warm.
Nutrition:
Calories
215 kcal
Fat 8.9 g
Carbohydrates 27.4g
Protein 6.3 g
Cholesterol 40 mg
Sodium
325 mg

Wheat Bread

Preparation Time: 5 minutes
Total Time: 1 hour
Servings: 12
Ingredients:
2 1/2 C. whole wheat flour
1/2 C. bread flour
4 tbsp maple syrup
1/3 tsp salt
2 tbsp olive oil
1 1/4 C. water
1 1/2 tsp active dry yeast
Directions

In a bread machine pan, add all the ingredients in order as suggested by the manual.
Select the Wheat Bread cycle and press the Start button.
Nutrition:
Calories
144 kcal
Fat 2.8 g
Carbohydrates 26.9g
Protein 4.3 g
Cholesterol
0 mg
Sodium
67 mg

Italian Bread

Preparation Time: 1 h 30 minutes
Total Time: 2 hours 45 minutes
Servings: 9
Ingredients: 3/4 C. warm water
3 1/2 C. bread flour
2 tbsp warm water
1/2 C. white sugar
2 tbsp butter, softened
1 tbsp active dry yeast 2 eggs
2 tbsp lemon extract
Directions:
In a bread machine pan, place both quantities of warm water, butter, eggs, lemon extract, bread flour, sugar, and yeast in order as suggested by the manual.
Select the Dough cycle and press the Start button.
After the completion of cycle, place the dough onto a lightly floured surface.

Make 3 equal sized balls from the dough.

In the bottom of a greased cake pan, arrange the dough balls.

With a plastic wrap, cover the pan and keep aside in warm place for about 1 hour.

Meanwhile, set your oven to 350 degrees F.

Place the breads in the oven for about 15-20 minutes.

Enjoy.

Nutrition: Calories 283 kcal Fat 4.5 g Carbohydrates 50.4g Protein 8.2 g Cholesterol 43 mg Sodium 34 mg

order as suggested by the manual.

Select the White or Basic Bread cycle with Light Crust and press the Start button.

Just 5 minutes before the completion of cycle, add the chocolate chips and walnuts.

Nutrition:
Calories 290 kcal
Fat 12.8 g
Carbohydrates 40g
Protein 6.8 g
Cholesterol 1 mg
Sodium 271 mg

Sweet Buttermilk Bread

Preparation Time: 25 minutes
Total Time: 2 hours 28 minutes
Servings: 12

Ingredients: 1 C. water
2/3 C. chopped walnuts, toasted
3 tbsp powdered buttermilk
2/3 C. semisweet chocolate chips
5 tbsp margarine, softened
1 tsp salt
5 tbsp unsweetened cocoa powder
1/3 C. packed brown sugar
3 C. bread flour
2 1/4 tsp active dry yeast

Directions: In a bread machine pan, place all the ingredients except the chocolate chips and walnuts in

Panettone

Preparation Time: 5 minutes
Total Time: 3 hours 5 minutes
Servings: 6
Ingredients: 1 1/8 C. water
1 1/2 tbsp vegetable oil
2 tbsp brown sugar
3 1/4 C. bread flour
2 tbsp bread flour
3 tbsp dry milk powder
1 tbsp pumpkin pie spice
2 tsp active dry yeast
3/4 C. golden raisins
2 2/3 tbsp candied mixed fruit peel
Directions: In the pan of a bread machine, place the water, oil, brown sugar, bread flour, gluten flour, milk powder, mixed spice and yeast in order as suggested by the manual.
Select the Fruit or Basic White Bread cycle and press the Start button.
Just 5 minutes before the completion of cycle, add the fruit peel and raisins.
Transfer the bread onto a wire rack to cool before slicing.
Cut into desired sized slices and enjoy.
Nutrition: Calories 423 kcal
Fat 5 g Carbohydrates 81.8g
Protein 13.1 g
Cholesterol 1 mg
Sodium 26 mg

Orange Bread

Preparation Time: 30-45 minutes
Cooking Time: 30-45 minutes
Servings: 15

Ingredients:
1 egg
1 cup orange juice
1/4 cup hot water
1 tablespoon margarine
1/4 cup white sugar
3 1/2 cups bread flour
1 teaspoon salt
2 tablespoons orange zest
1 (.25 ounce) package active dry yeast
Directions:
Place ingredients into the pan of the bread machine in the order suggested by the manufacturer. Select the White Bread or Basic cycle, and Start.
Nutrition:
Calories: 34
Calories
Total Fat: 1.1 g
Cholesterol: 12 mg
Sodium: 168 mg
Total Carbohydrate: 5.5 g
Protein: 0.7 g

Orange Ginger Bread

Preparation Time: 10 minutes
Cooking Time: 25 minutes
Servings: 12
Ingredients:
1 cup orange juice
3 tablespoons butter
3 tablespoons brown sugar
1 teaspoon ground cinnamon
1 1/2 teaspoons ground ginger
1/8 teaspoon salt
1 1/2 cups all-purpose flour
1 1/2 cups whole wheat flour
1 1/2 teaspoons active dry yeast
Directions:

Place ingredients into the bread machine in the order recommended by the manufacturer. Select the Dough cycle, and press Start. When the machine signals the end of the cycle, remove the dough. Roll into a loaf, and place in a 9x5 inch bread pan. Set aside to rise until doubled, or until your finger leaves a dent when the dough is pressed lightly.

Preheat the oven to 350 degrees F (175 degrees C). Bake the bread for 25 minutes in the preheated oven, or until a rich golden brown. Nutrition: Calories: 158 Calories Total Fat: 3.4 g Cholesterol: 8 mg Sodium: 47 mg Total Carbohydrate: 28.8 g Protein: 4.1 g

Panettone II

Preparation Time: 5 minutes
Cooking Time: 3 hours
Servings: 10
Ingredients:
3/4 cup warm water
1/4 cup butter
2 eggs
1 1/2 teaspoons vanilla extract
3 1/4 cups bread flour
2 tablespoons white sugar
2 tablespoons dry milk powder
1 1/2 teaspoons salt
2 teaspoons bread machine yeast
1/2 cup chopped dried mixed fruit
Directions:

Place all of the ingredients except for the mixed fruit into the pan of your bread machine in order directed by manufacturer. Select Sweet or Basic/White bread cycle, and use the Medium or Light crust color. Do not use the delay cycles. Add the fruit 5 to 10 minutes before the last kneading cycle ends, or when the raisin or nut signal starts. Nutrition: Calories: 93 Calories Total Fat: 5.7 g Cholesterol: 50 mg Sodium: 405 mg Total Carbohydrate: 8.7 g Protein: 2.3 g

Portuguese Sweet Bread I

Preparation Time: 5 minutes
Cooking Time: 3 hours
Servings: 12
Ingredients:
1 cup milk
1 egg
2 tablespoons margarine
1/3 cup white sugar
3/4 teaspoon salt
3 cups bread flour
2 1/2 teaspoons active dry yeast
Directions:
Add ingredients in order suggested by your manufacturer.
Select "sweet bread" setting.
Nutrition:
Calories: 56
Calories

Total Fat: 2.6 g
Cholesterol: 17 mg
Sodium: 181 mg
Total Carbohydrate: 6.9 g
Protein: 1.5 g

Pumpkin Yeast Bread

Preparation Time: 20 minutes
Cooking Time: 1-2 hours
Servings: 12
Ingredients:
5/8 cup warm water
1/2 cup canned pumpkin puree
1/4 cup margarine
1/4 cup nonfat dry milk powder
1/4 cup packed brown sugar
1 teaspoon ground cinnamon
3/4 teaspoon ground nutmeg
3/4 teaspoon salt
1/8 teaspoon ground ginger
2 3/4 cups bread flour
2 1/4 teaspoons active dry yeast
Directions:
Place ingredients in bread machine pan in the order suggested by the manufacturer. Select basic setting. Start.
To bake bread in oven: select dough or manual cycle. Once cycle is complete, shape dough and place in a greased loaf pan. Allow to rise in a warm spot until doubled in size. Bake in a preheated 350 degrees F (175 degrees C) oven for 35 to 45 minutes or until a thermometer inserted in the center of the loaf reads 200 degrees F (95 degrees C).

Nutrition:
Calories: 67
Calories
Total Fat: 3.9 g
Cholesterol: < 1 mg
Sodium: 229 mg
Total Carbohydrate: 7.2 g
Protein: 1.4 g

Raisin Bread II

Preparation Time: 5 minutes
Cooking Time: 3 hours
Servings: 12
Ingredients:
1 cup warm water (110 degrees F/45 degrees C)
1 1/2 tablespoons lard
2 teaspoons active dry yeast
1/2 cup raisins
3 cups bread flour
1 teaspoon salt
1 teaspoon ground cinnamon
Directions:
Place ingredients in the bread machine pan in the order suggested by the manufacture Select the Basic or White Bread setting. There is no need to select Fruit Bread setting, nor to add the raisins in later. Start the machine. After first knead, bread should be smooth, elastic, and dry to touch. Adjust if necessary with additional flour.
After baking, remove pan immediately. Rest for 10 minutes in the pan. Remove bread from the pan, and cool on a wire rack for 10 minutes before serving.
Nutrition:
Calories: 159

Calories
Total Fat: 2.2 g
Cholesterol: 2 mg
Sodium: 195 mg
Total Carbohydrate: 30 g
Protein: 4.6 g

Cholesterol: 25 mg
Sodium: 252 mg
Total Carbohydrate: 27.3 g
Protein: 4.7 g

Rum Raisin Bread

Preparation Time: 15 minutes
Cooking Time: 40 minutes
Servings: 10

Ingredients:

2 tablespoons rum
1/2 cup raisins
1/2 cup water
2 cups bread flour
1 tablespoon dry milk powder
2 teaspoons brown sugar
1 teaspoon salt
2 teaspoons butter
2 tablespoons heavy whipping cream
1/2 teaspoon rum flavored extract
1 egg
1 teaspoon olive oil
1 1/2 teaspoons active dry yeast

Directions:

In a small bowl, pour rum over raisins. Let stand for 30 minutes and drain.

Place ingredients in pan in the order recommended by the manufacturer. Use the regular setting for a 1 pound loaf.

If your machine has a Fruit setting, add the raisins at the signal, or about 5 minutes before the kneading cycle has finished.

Nutrition: Calories: 164
Calories Total Fat: 3.4 g

Soft Moist and Gooey Cinnamon Buns

Preparation Time: 15 minutes
Cooking Time: 20 minutes
Servings: 24

Ingredients:

1 cup milk
1 egg, beaten
4 tablespoons melted butter
4 tablespoons water
1/2 (3.5 ounce) package instant vanilla pudding mix
4 cups bread flour
1 tablespoon white sugar
1/2 teaspoon salt
2 1/4 teaspoons bread machine yeast
1/2 cup butter, softened
1 cup packed brown sugar
2 teaspoons ground cinnamon
1/4 cup chopped walnuts (optional)
1/4 cup raisins (optional)
1 teaspoon milk
1 1/2 cups confectioners' sugar
4 tablespoons butter, softened
1 teaspoon vanilla extract

Directions:

In a bread machine pan, place the milk, beaten egg, melted butter, water, vanilla pudding mix, bread flour, sugar, salt and yeast in the order recommended by the manufacturer. Select the Dough cycle.
When cycle is finished, remove the dough, and knead for 3 to 5 minutes. Roll out to a large rectangle.
Mix together the softened butter, brown sugar and cinnamon. Spread over dough.

Sprinkle with chopped walnuts and raisins, if desired. Starting with the widest end, roll the dough into a log. Pinch to seal seams. Cut into 1/2 inch to 1 inch slices, and place in a greased 9x13 inch pan. Place in a draft-free space, and allow to rise until doubled.
Preheat the oven to 350 degrees F (175 degrees C). Bake for 15 to 20 minutes. To make frosting, mix the milk, confectioners' sugar, softened butter and vanilla in a small bowl. Spread over warm cinnamon rolls.

Nutrition:
Calories: 165
Calories
Total Fat: 8.9 g
Cholesterol: 29 mg
Sodium: 143 mg
Total Carbohydrate: 21.2 g
Protein: 1.1 g

Strawberry Oatmeal Cream Cheese Bread

Preparation Time: 30-45 minutes
Cooking Time: 30-45 minutes

Servings: 10
Ingredients:
1/3 cup milk
1/3 cup strawberries, mashed
1/3 cup cream cheese, diced
1 tablespoon butter
2 tablespoons honey
1 teaspoon salt
1/2 cup rolled oats
1 1/2 cups bread flour
1 1/2 teaspoons active dry yeast
Directions:
Place ingredients in the pan of the bread machine in the order suggested by the manufacturer. Start.
Nutrition: Calories: 73
Calories Total Fat: 4.3 g
Cholesterol: 12 mg
Sodium: 268 mg
Total Carbohydrate: 7.4 g
Protein: 1.7 g

Tangy Cranberry Bread

Preparation Time: 10 minutes
Cooking Time: 30 minutes
Servings: 15
Ingredients:
1 1/4 cups cranberry juice
3 cups bread flour
2 tablespoons dry milk powder
1 1/2 teaspoons salt
2 tablespoons butter, softened
3 tablespoons orange marmalade
1/3 cup dried cranberries
1 tablespoon active dry yeast
Directions:
Place all ingredients (except cranberries) in the bread machine according to manufacturer's instructions. If using the delayed time cycle, place dried cranberries away from water. Press start.
If your machine has a Fruit setting, add the cranberries at the signal, or about 5 minutes before the kneading cycle has finished.
Nutrition:
Calories: 49
Calories
Total Fat: 1.6 g
Cholesterol: 4 mg
Sodium: 252 mg
Total Carbohydrate: 8.5 g
Protein: 0.7 g

100 Whole Wheat Peanut Butter and Jelly Bread

Preparation Time: 10 minutes
Cooking Time: 40 minutes
Servings: 12
Ingredients:
10 ounces water
1/2 cup peanut butter
1/2 cup strawberry jelly
1 1/2 tablespoons light brown sugar
1/2 teaspoon salt
3/4 teaspoon baking soda
3/4 teaspoon baking powder
3 tablespoons vital wheat gluten
3 1/3 cups whole wheat flour
1 tablespoon whole wheat flour
1 1/2 teaspoons active dry yeast
Directions:

Place water, peanut butter, jelly, brown sugar, salt, baking soda, baking powder, gluten, 3 1/3 cups plus 1 tablespoon whole wheat flour, and yeast, respectively, in the pan of a bread machine. Select 1 1/2 Pound Loaf, Medium Crust, Wheat cycle, and press Start.
Nutrition:
Calories: 230
Calories
Total Fat: 6.1 g
Cholesterol: 0 mg
Sodium: 259 mg
Total Carbohydrate: 38.6 g
Protein: 8.7 g

Bread Machine Ezekiel Bread

Preparation Time: 15 minutes
Cooking Time: 40 minutes
Servings: 10
Ingredients:
1/2 cup milk
1/2 cup water
1 egg
2 1/2 tablespoons olive oil, divided
1 tablespoon honey
1 tablespoon dry black beans
1 tablespoon dry lentils
1 tablespoon dry kidney beans
1 tablespoon barley
1 cup unbleached all-purpose flour
1 cup whole wheat flour
1/4 cup millet flour
1/4 cup rye flour
1/4 cup cracked wheat
2 tablespoons wheat germ
1 teaspoon salt
2 teaspoons bread machine yeast
Directions:
Place milk and water into a microwave-safe glass measuring cup. Heat in microwave for 35 seconds. Pour mixture into bread machine. Add egg, 2 tablespoons olive oil, and honey.
Grind black beans, lentils, kidney beans, and barley in a coffee grinder until fine. Combine grounds, unbleached flour, whole wheat flour, millet flour, rye flour, cracked wheat, wheat germ, and salt in the bread machine. Add yeast. Set bread machine on dough cycle.
Remove and punch down dough once bread machine beeps. Roll dough out onto a pastry cloth. Grease a loaf pan with remaining olive oil. Shape dough into a loaf and place into the prepared pan. Cover with a damp cloth and let rise until doubled in volume, about 40 minutes. Preheat oven to 375 degrees F (190 degrees C).
Uncover dough and bake in the preheated oven for 10 minutes. Lower oven temperature to 350 degrees F (175 degrees C)
bake until browned, 30 to 35 minutes more. Let bread rest in the pan for 10 minutes remove and let cool until ready to slice.
Nutrition:

Calories: 192
Calories
Total Fat: 5 g
Cholesterol: 20 mg
Sodium: 247 mg
Total Carbohydrate: 31.5 g
Protein: 6.6 g

Bread Machine Honey Oat Wheat Bread

Preparation Time: 10 minutes
Cooking Time: 35 minutes
Servings: 12

Ingredients:
2 1/2 teaspoons active dry yeast
2 tablespoons white sugar
1 1/2 cups warm water (110 degrees F/45 degrees C)
3 cups all-purpose flour
1 cup whole wheat flour
1 cup rolled oats
3 tablespoons powdered milk
1 teaspoon salt
1/4 cup honey
1/4 cup vegetable oil
3 tablespoons butter, softened
Cooking spray

Directions:
Place the yeast, sugar, and water in the pan of a bread machine. Allow yeast to dissolve and foam, about 10 minutes. Meanwhile, mix the all-purpose flour, whole wheat flour, rolled oats, powdered milk, and salt in a bowl set aside. Add the honey, vegetable oil, and butter to the yeast mixture, and pour the flour mixture on top.
Select the Dough cycle press start. Allow the bread machine to complete the cycle, about 1 1/2 hours, then transfer the dough to a 9x5-inch loaf pan sprayed with cooking spray. Allow the bread to rise for 1 hour in a warm place.
Preheat oven to 375 degrees F (190 degrees C).
Bake in the preheated oven until the top is golden brown, about 35 minutes.
Nutrition:
Calories: 281
Calories
Total Fat: 8.9 g
Cholesterol: 10 mg
Sodium: 225 mg
Total Carbohydrate: 44.7 g
Protein: 6.4 g

Butter Honey Wheat Bread

Preparation Time: 5 minutes
Cooking Time: 3 hours
Servings: 12

Ingredients:
1 cup water
2 tablespoons margarine
2 tablespoons honey
2 cups bread flour
1/2 cup whole wheat flour
1/3 cup dry milk powder
1 teaspoon salt
1 (.25 ounce) package active dry yeast

Directions:
Put ingredients into bread machine in the order suggested by the manufacturer.
Process for large (1-1/2 pound) loaf, wheat setting.
Nutrition:
Calories: 57
Calories
Total Fat: 1.9 g
Cholesterol: < 1 mg
Sodium: 234 mg

Total Carbohydrate: 8.5 g
Protein: 2.1 g

Buttermilk Bread I

Preparation Time: 30-45
minutes
Cooking Time: 1 hour
Servings: 12

Ingredients:
1 1/2 cups buttermilk
1 1/2 tablespoons margarine
2 tablespoons white sugar
1 teaspoon salt
3 cups bread flour
1 1/3 cups whole wheat flour
2 1/4 teaspoons active dry
yeast

Directions:
Place buttermilk, butter or
margarine, sugar, salt, flour,
whole wheat flour, and yeast
into pan of bread machine.
Bake on White Bread setting.
Cool on wire racks before
slicing.
Nutrition: Calories: 80
Calories
Total Fat: 1.9 g
Cholesterol: 1 mg
Sodium: 243 mg
Total Carbohydrate: 13.5 g
Protein: 3.1 g

Chapter 12 Meat

French Ham Bread
Preparation Time: 30-45 minutes
Cooking Time: 2 hours
Servings: 8
Ingredients:
3 1/3 cups wheat flour
1 cup ham
½ cup milk powder
1 ½ tablespoons sugar
1 teaspoon yeast, fresh
1 teaspoon salt
1 teaspoon dried basil
1 1/3 cups water
2 tablespoons olive oil
Directions:
Cut ham into cubes of 0.5-1 cm (approximately ¼ inch).
Put the ingredients in the bread maker in the following order: water, olive oil, salt, sugar, flour, milk powder, ham, and yeast.
Put all the ingredients according to the instructions to your bread maker.
Basil put in a dispenser or fill it later, at the signal in the container.
Turn on the bread maker.
After the end of the baking cycle, leave the bread container in the bread maker to keep warm for 1 hour.
Then your delicious bread is ready!
Nutrition: Calories 287
Total Fat 5.5g
Saturated Fat 1.1g
Cholesterol 11g
Sodium 557mg
Total Carbohydrate 47.2g
Dietary Fiber 1.7g
Total Sugars 6.4g
Protein 11.4g

Meat Bread
Preparation Time: 1 hour 30 minutes
Cooking Time: 1 hour 30 minutes
Servings: 8
Ingredients:
2 cups boiled chicken
1 cup milk   3 cups flour
1 tablespoon dry yeast   1 egg
1 teaspoon sugar
½ tablespoon salt
2 tablespoons oil
Directions:
Pre-cook the meat. You can use a leg or fillet.
Separate the meat from the bone and cut into small pieces.
Pour all ingredients into the bread maker according to the instructions.
Add chicken pieces now.
The program is Basic.
This bread is perfectly combined with dill and butter.
Nutrition: Calories 283
Total Fat 6.2g
Saturated Fat 1.4g
Cholesterol 50g

Sodium 484mg
Total Carbohydrate 38.4g
Dietary Fiber 1.6g
Total Sugars 2g
Protein 17.2g

Onion Bacon Bread

Preparation Time: 1 hour 30 minutes
Cooking Time: 1 hour 30 minutes
Servings: 8

Ingredients:
1 ½ cups water
2 tablespoons sugar
3 teaspoons dry yeast
4 ½ cups flour
1 egg
2 teaspoons salt
1 tablespoon oil
3 small onions, chopped
1 cup bacon

Directions:
Cut the bacon.
Put all the ingredients into the bread machine.
Set it to the Basic program.
Enjoy this tasty bread!
Nutrition:
Calories 391
Total Fat 9.7g
Saturated Fat 2.7g
Cholesterol 38g
Sodium 960mg
Total Carbohydrate 59.9g
Dietary Fiber 2.8g
Total Sugars 4.3g
Protein 14.7g

Fish Bell Pepper Bran Bread

Preparation Time: 1 hour 30 minutes
Cooking Time: 1 hour 30 minutes
Servings: 8

Ingredients
2 ½ cups flour
½ cup bran
1 1/3 cups water
1 ½ teaspoons salt
1 ½ teaspoons sugar
1 ½ tablespoon mustard oil
1 ¼ teaspoons dry yeast
2 teaspoons powdered milk
1 cup chopped bell pepper
¾ cup chopped smoked fish
1 onion

Directions:
Grind onion and fry until golden brown.
Cut the fish into small pieces and the pepper into cubes.
Load all the ingredients in the bucket.
Turn on the baking program.
Bon Appetit!
Nutrition:
Calories 208
Total Fat 3.8g
Saturated Fat 0.5g
Cholesterol 8g
Sodium 487mg
Total Carbohydrate 35.9g
Dietary Fiber 4.2g
Total Sugars 2.7g
Protein 7.2g

Sausage Bread

Preparation Time: 2 hours
Cooking Time: 2 hours
Servings: 8

Ingredients:
1 ½ teaspoons dry yeast

3 cups flour
1 teaspoon sugar
1 ½ teaspoons salt
1 1/3 cups whey
1 tablespoon oil
1 cup chopped smoked sausage

Directions:
Fold all the ingredients in the order that is recommended specifically for your model.
Set the required parameters for baking bread.
When ready, remove the delicious hot bread.
Wait for it to cool down and enjoy with sausage.
Nutrition:
Calories 234
Total Fat 5.1g
Saturated Fat 1.2g
Cholesterol 9g
Sodium 535mg
Total Carbohydrate 38.7g
Dietary Fiber 1.4g
Total Sugars 2.7g
Protein 7.4g

Cheese Sausage Bread

Preparation Time: 2 hours
Cooking Time: 2 hours
Servings: 8

Ingredients
1 teaspoon dry yeast
3 ½ cups flour
1 teaspoon salt
1 tablespoon sugar
1 ½ tablespoon oil
2 tablespoons smoked sausage
2 tablespoons grated cheese
1 tablespoon chopped garlic
1 cup water

Directions:
Cut the sausage into small cubes.
Grate the cheese on a grater chop the garlic.
Add the ingredients to the bread machine according to the instructions.
Turn on the baking program, and let it do the work.
Nutrition:
Calories 260
Total Fat 5.6g
Saturated Fat 1.4g
Cholesterol 8g
Sodium 355mg
Total Carbohydrate 43.8g
Dietary Fiber 1.6g
Total Sugars 1.7g
Protein 7.7g

Cheesy Pizza Dough

Preparation Time: 20 minutes
Cooking Time: 1 hour 30 minutes
Serving: 4

Ingredients:
1/2 cup warm beer, or more as needed
1 tbsp. Parmesan cheese
1 1/2 tsps. pizza dough yeast
1 tsp. salt
1 tsp. ground black pepper
1 tsp. granulated garlic
1 tbsp. olive oil
1 1/4 cups all-purpose flour, or more as needed

Directions:
In a big mixing bowl, mix granulated garlic, pepper, salt, yeast, Parmesan cheese, and beer. Mix until salt dissolves. Allow mixture to stand for 10-

20 minutes until yeast creates a creamy layer. Mix in olive oil.

Mix flour in yeast mixture until dough becomes smooth. Add small amounts of flour or beer if the dough is too sticky or dry. Let rise for an hour. Punch dough down and roll out into a pizza crust on a work surface that's floured.
Nutrition: Calories: 199
Total Carbohydrate: 32.4 g
Cholesterol: 1 mg
Total Fat: 4.2 g
Protein: 5.4 g
Sodium: 604 mg

Collards & Bacon Grilled Pizza

Preparation Time: 15 minutes
Cooking Time: 15 minutes
Serving: 4

Ingredients:
1 lb. whole-wheat pizza dough
3 tbsps. garlic-flavored olive oil
2 cups thinly sliced cooked collard greens
1 cup shredded Cheddar cheese
¼ cup crumbled cooked bacon

Directions:
Heat grill to medium-high. Roll out dough to an oval that's 12 inches on a surface that's lightly floured. Move to a big baking sheet that's lightly floured. Put Cheddar, collards, oil, and dough on the grill.
Grease grill rack. Move crust to grill. Close lid and cook for

1-2 minutes until light brown and puffed. Use tongs to flip over the crust. Spread oil on the crust and top with Cheddar and collards. Close lid and cook until cheese melts for another 2-3 minutes or the crust is light brown at the bottom.
Put pizza on baking sheet and top using bacon.
Nutrition: Calories: 498
Total Carbohydrate: 50 g
Cholesterol: 33 mg
Total Fat: 28 g Fiber: 6 g
Protein: 19 g Sodium: 573 mg
Sugar: 3 g Saturated Fat: 7 g

Crazy Crust Pizza Dough

Preparation Time: 10 minutes
Cooking Time: 45 minutes
Serving: 8

Ingredients:
1 cup all-purpose flour
1 tsp. salt
1 tsp. dried oregano
1/8 tsp. black pepper
2 eggs, lightly beaten
2/3 cup milk

Directions:
Heat oven to 200 degrees C or 400 degrees F. Grease a baking sheet or rimmed pizza pan lightly.
Mix black pepper, oregano, salt, and flour in a big bowl. Stir in milk and eggs thoroughly. Put batter in the pan and tilt it until it is evenly coated. Put whatever toppings you want on top of the batter.

Bake it in the oven until the crust is set for 20-25 minutes. Take crust out of the oven. Drizzle pizza sauce on and top with cheese. Bake for around 10 minutes until the cheese melts.
Nutrition:
Calories: 86
Total Carbohydrate: 13.1 g
Cholesterol: 48 mg
Total Fat: 1.8 g
Protein: 3.9 g
Sodium: 317 mg

Deep Dish Pizza Dough

Preparation Time: 15 minutes
Cooking Time: 2 hours 15 minutes
Serving: 8
Ingredients:
1 (.25 oz.) package active dry yeast
1/3 cup white sugar
2/3 cup water
2 cups all-purpose flour
1 cup bread flour
1/4 cup corn oil
2 tsps. salt
6 tbsps. vegetable oil
1/2 cup all-purpose flour, or as needed

Directions:
Dissolve sugar and yeast in a bowl with water. Let the mixture stand for 5 minutes until the yeast starts to form creamy foam and softens.
In a bowl, mix bread flour, salt, corn oil, and 2 cups of all-purpose flour. Add the yeast mixture. Knead the mixture in a work surface using 1/2 of the all-purpose flour until well-incorporated. Place the dough in a warm area and let it rise for 2 hours until its size doubles.
Nutrition: Calories: 328
Total Carbohydrate: 38.5 g
Cholesterol: 0 mg
Total Fat: 17.5 g Protein: 4.4 g
Sodium: 583 mg

Double Crust Stuffed Pizza

Preparation Time: 30 minutes
Cooking Time: 2 hours 45 minutes
Serving: 8
Ingredients:
1 1/2 tsps. white sugar
1 cup warm water (100 degrees F/40 degrees C)
1 1/2 tsps. active dry yeast
1 tbsp. olive oil
1/2 tsp. salt
2 cups all-purpose flour
1 (8 oz.) can crushed tomatoes
1 tbsp. packed brown sugar
1/2 tsp. garlic powder
1 tsp. olive oil
1/2 tsp. salt
3 cups shredded mozzarella cheese, divided
1/2 lb. bulk Italian sausage
1 (4 oz.) package sliced pepperoni
1 (8 oz.) package sliced fresh mushrooms
1/2 green bell pepper, chopped
1/2 red bell pepper, chopped
Directions:

In a large bowl or work bowl of a stand mixer, mix warm water and white sugar. Sprinkle with yeast and let the mixture stand for 5 minutes until the yeast starts to form creamy foam and softens. Stir in 1 tbsp. of olive oil.

Mix flour with 1/2 tsp. of salt. Add half of the flour mixture into the yeast mixture and mix until no dry spots are visible. Whisk in remaining flour, a half cup at a time, mixing well every after addition. Place the dough in a lightly floured surface once it has pulled together. Knead the dough for 8 minutes until elastic and smooth. You can use the dough hook in a stand mixer to mix the dough.

Transfer the dough into a lightly oiled large bowl and flip to coat the dough with oil. Use a light cloth to cover the dough. Let it rise in a warm place for 1 hour until the volume doubles.

In a small saucepan, mix 1 tsp. of olive oil, brown sugar, crushed tomatoes, garlic powder, and salt. Cover the saucepan and let it cook over low heat for 30 minutes until the tomatoes begin to break down.

Set the oven to 450°F (230°C) for preheating. Flatten the dough and place it in a lightly floured surface. Divide the dough into 2 equal portions. Roll one portion into a 12-inches thin circle. Roll the other portion into a 9-inches thicker circle.

Press the12-inches dough round into an ungreased 9-inches springform pan. Top the dough with a cup of cheese. Form sausage into a 9-inches patty and place it on top of the cheese. Arrange pepperoni, green pepper, mushrooms, red pepper, and remaining cheese on top of the sausage patty. Place the 9-inches dough round on top, pinching its edges to seal. Make vent holes on top of the crust by cutting several 1/2-inch on top. Pour the sauce evenly on top of the crust, leaving only 1/2-inch border at the edges.

Bake the pizza inside the preheated oven for 40-45 minutes until the cheese is melted, the sausage is cooked through, and the crust is fixed. Let the pizza rest for 15 minutes. Before serving, cut the pizza into wedges.

Nutrition:

Calories: 410

Total Carbohydrate: 32.5 g

Cholesterol: 53 mg

Total Fat: 21.1 g

Protein: 22.2 g

Sodium: 1063 mg

Chapter 13 Vegetables

Carrot Bread

Preparation Time: 30-45 minutes

Cooking Time: 2 hours 10 minutes

Servings: Makes 1 loaf

Ingredients:

4 whole eggs

¼ teaspoon sea salt

½ cup (100 g, 4 oz) butter, melted

½ cup (120 g, 4 oz) brown sugar

1 tablespoon vanilla sugar

2 teaspoon ground cinnamon

3 cups (350 g, 13.50 oz) white bread flour

1 tablespoon baking powder

¼ cup (50 g) ground nuts

¾ cup (150 g) carrot, grated

Directions:

Prepare all of the ingredients for your bread and measuring means (a cup, a spoon, kitchen scales).

Carefully measure the ingredients into the pan, except the carrots and nuts.

Place all of the ingredients into the bread bucket in the right order, following the manual for your bread machine.

Close the cover.

Select the program of your bread machine to CAKE and choose the crust color to LIGHT.

Press START.

After the signal, put the grated carrots and nuts to the dough. Wait until the program completes.

When done, take the bucket out and let it cool for 5-10 minutes.

Shake the loaf from the pan and let cool for 30 minutes on a cooling rack.

Cover the prepared bread with icing sugar.

Slice, serve and enjoy the taste of fragrant homemade bread.

Nutrition:

Calories 398, Total Fat 17.3 g, Saturated Fat 8.3 g, Cholesterol 112 mg sodium202 mg, Total Carbohydrate 53 g, Dietary Fiber 2.9 g

Total Sugars 14 g

protein 9.2 g, Vitamin D 16 mcg, Calcium 132 mg, Iron 3 mg, Potassium 381 mg

Spinach Bread

Preparation Time: 30-45 minutes

Cooking Time: 3 ½ hours

Servings: 2 pounds / 20 slices

Ingredients:

4 cups bread flour, sifted

½ cup frozen spinach

1 cup lukewarm water (80 degrees F)

1 tablespoon olive oil

1½ teaspoon active dry yeast

Directions:

Defrost the spinach.

Prepare all of the ingredients for your bread and measuring means (a cup, a spoon, kitchen scales).

Carefully measure the ingredients into the pan, except the spinach.

Place all of the ingredients into the bread bucket in the right order, following the manual for your bread machine.

Close the cover.

Select the program of your bread machine to BASIC and choose the crust color to MEDIUM.

Press START.

After the signal, put the spinach to the dough.

Wait until the program completes.

When done, take the bucket out and let it cool for 5-10 minutes.

Shake the loaf from the pan and let cool for 30 minutes on a cooling rack.

Slice, serve and enjoy the taste of fragrant homemade bread.

Nutrition:

Calories 238

Total Fat 1.7g

Saturated Fat 0.2g

Cholesterol 0g

Sodium 3mg

Total Carbohydrate 44.4g

Dietary Fiber 0.2g

Total Sugars 2g

Protein 8.3g

Mushroom Bread

Preparation Time: 30-45 minutes
Cooking Time: 3 ½ hours
Servings: 2 pounds / 20 slices
Ingredients:
4 cups all-purpose flour
½ cup lukewarm water (80 degrees F)
1 cup your favorite mushrooms, dried
1 tablespoon melted butter
2 teaspoons white sugar
2 egg yolks, lightly beaten
1 teaspoon active dry yeast
1 teaspoon sea salt
Directions:
Put the mushrooms to the 200 ml of boiling water. Leave for 1 hour, drain (and keep) the broth.
Finely chop the mushrooms.
Prepare all of the ingredients for your bread and measuring means (a cup, a spoon, kitchen scales).
Carefully measure the ingredients into the pan.
Place all of the ingredients, including the mushroom broth, into the bread bucket in the right order, following the manual for your bread machine.
Close the cover.
Select the program of your bread machine to BASIC and choose the crust color to MEDIUM.
Press START.
Wait until the program completes.

When done, take the bucket out and let it cool for 5-10 minutes.
Shake the loaf from the pan and let cool for 30 minutes on a cooling rack.
Slice, serve and enjoy the taste of fragrant homemade bread.
Nutrition:
Calories 261
Total Fat 3.2g
Saturated Fat 1.4g
Cholesterol 56g
Sodium 305mg
Total Carbohydrate 49.3g
Dietary Fiber 1.9g
Total Sugars 1.3g
Protein 7.6g

Cheese Broccoli Cauliflower Bread

Preparation Time: 30 minutes
Cooking Time: 3 hours 10 minutes
Servings: Makes 1 loaf
Ingredients:
¼ cup lukewarm water (80 degrees F)
4 tablespoons extra virgin olive oil
1 egg white
1 teaspoon fresh lemon juice
2/3 cup cheddar cheese, grated
3 tablespoons green onion
½ cup broccoli, chopped
½ cup cauliflower, chopped
½ teaspoon lemon pepper seasoning
2 cups bread flour
1 teaspoon active dry yeast
Directions:
Prepare all of the ingredients for your bread and measuring

means (a cup, a spoon, kitchen scales).

Carefully measure the ingredients into the pan, except the vegetables and cheese.

Place all of the ingredients into the bread bucket in the right order, following the manual for your bread machine.

Close the cover.

Select the program of your bread machine to BASIC and choose the crust color to MEDIUM.

Press START.

After the signal, put the vegetables and cheese to the dough.

Wait until the program completes.

When done, take the bucket out and let it cool for 5-10 minutes.

Shake the loaf from the pan and let cool for 30 minutes on a cooling rack.

Slice, serve and enjoy the taste of fragrant homemade bread.

Nutrition:
Calories 220
Total Fat 10.5g
Saturated Fat 3.1g
Cholesterol 10g
Sodium 68mg
Total Carbohydrate 25.2g
Dietary Fiber 1.4g
Total Sugars 0.5g
Protein 6.6g, Vitamin D 1mcg,
Calcium 80mg, Iron 2mg,
Potassium 105mg

Potato Rosemary Bread

Preparation Time: 30 minutes
Cooking Time: 30 minutes
Servings: Makes 1 loaf
Ingredients:
4 cups bread flour, sifted
1 tablespoon white sugar
1 tablespoon sunflower oil
1½ teaspoons salt
1½ cups lukewarm water
1 teaspoon active dry yeast
1 cup potatoes, mashed
2 teaspoons crushed rosemary
Directions:
Prepare all of the ingredients for your bread and measuring means (a cup, a spoon, kitchen scales).

Carefully measure the ingredients into the pan, except the potato and rosemary.

Place all of the ingredients into the bread bucket in the right order, following the manual for your bread machine.

Close the cover.

Select the program of your bread machine to BREAD with FILLINGS and choose the crust color to MEDIUM.

Press START.

After the signal, put the mashed potato and rosemary to the dough.

Wait until the program completes.

When done, take the bucket out and let it cool for 5-10 minutes.

Shake the loaf from the pan and let cool for 30 minutes on a cooling rack.

Slice, serve and enjoy the taste of fragrant homemade bread.

Nutrition:

Calories 106
Total Fat 1g
Saturated Fat 0.1g
Cholesterol 0g
Sodium 641mg
Total Carbohydrate 21g
Dietary Fiber 1g
Total Sugars 0.8g
Protein 2.9g, Vitamin D 0mcg,
Calcium 7mg, Iron 1mg,
Potassium 63mg

Parsley Garlic Bread

Preparation Time: 30 minutes
Cooking Time: 30 minutes
Servings: Makes 1 loaf

Ingredients:

16 slice bread (2 pounds)
1⅓ cups lukewarm milk
2 tablespoons unsalted butter, melted
4 teaspoons sugar
2 teaspoons table salt
2⅔ teaspoons garlic powder
2⅔ teaspoons fresh parsley, chopped
4 cups white bread flour
2¼ teaspoons bread machine yeast
12 slice bread (1½ pounds)
1 cup lukewarm milk
1½ tablespoons unsalted butter, melted
1 tablespoon sugar
1½ teaspoons table salt
2 teaspoons garlic powder
2 teaspoons fresh parsley, chopped
3 cups white bread flour
1¾ teaspoons bread machine yeast

Directions:

Choose the size of loaf you would like to make and measure your ingredients.

Add the ingredients to the bread pan in the order listed above.
Place the pan in the bread machine and close the lid.
Turn on the bread maker.
Select the White/Basic setting, then the loaf size, and finally the crust color. Start the cycle.
When the cycle is finished and the bread is baked, carefully remove the pan from the machine. Use a pot holder as the handle will be very hot. Let rest for a few minutes.
Remove the bread from the pan and allow to cool on a wire rack for at least 10 minutes before slicing.
Nutrition:
Calories 143 fat 2.2 g
carbs 24.6 g sodium317 mg
protein 4.3 g

Swiss Olive Bread

Preparation Time: 30 minutes
Cooking Time: 30 minutes
Servings: Makes 1 loaf
Ingredients:
16 slice bread (2 pounds)
1⅓ cups lukewarm milk
2 tablespoons unsalted butter, melted
1⅓ teaspoons minced garlic
2 tablespoons sugar
1⅓ teaspoons table salt
1 cup Swiss cheese, shredded
4 cups white bread flour
1½ teaspoons bread machine yeast
½ cup chopped black olives
12 slice bread (1½ pounds)
1 cup lukewarm milk
1½ tablespoons unsalted butter, melted
1 teaspoon minced garlic
1½ tablespoons sugar
1 teaspoon table salt
¾ cup Swiss cheese, shredded
3 cups white bread flour
1 teaspoon bread machine yeast
⅓ cup chopped black olives
Directions:
Choose the size of loaf you would like to make and measure your ingredients.
Add all of the ingredients except for the olives to the bread pan in the order listed above.
Place the pan in the bread machine and close the lid.
Turn on the bread maker.
Select the White/Basic or Fruit/Nut (if your machine has this setting) setting, then the loaf size, and finally the crust color. Start the cycle.
When the machine signals to add ingredients, add the olives. (Some machines have a fruit/nut hopper where you can add the olives when you start the machine. The machine will automatically add them to the dough during the baking process.)
When the cycle is finished and the bread is baked, carefully remove the pan from the machine. Use a pot holder as the handle will be very hot. Let rest for a few minutes.
Remove the bread from the pan and allow to cool on a

wire rack for at least 10 minutes before slicing.
Nutrition: Calories 147 fat 4.8 g carbs 26.7 g sodium263 mg protein 5.8 g

Broccoli Rice Pizza Crust

Preparation Time: 25 minutes
Cooking Time: 1 hour 30 minutes
Serving: 4

Ingredients:
1 (12 oz.) bag broccoli florets
1 tsp. sea salt
1/2 cup packed finely grated Parmesan cheese
1 egg
2 tbsps. Italian bread crumbs
2 cloves garlic, grated
1 tsp. dried oregano
1 pinch red pepper flakes (optional)
1 1/2 tsps. olive oil, or as needed
sea salt

Direction:
Set the oven to 425°F (220°C) for preheating. Use a parchment paper to line the baking sheet.
In a food processor, pulse 1/2 of the broccoli 20 times until its texture resembles rice. Do the same with the remaining half of the broccoli.
Pour salt and 1/2-inch of water in a large shallow saucepan and boil it over high heat. Adjust the heat to low, and then add the broccoli rice. Cover the saucepan and let it simmer for 5 minutes until tender. Let it drain and cool for 10 minutes. Transfer the broccoli rice into the center of a dish towel. Wrap the towel and twist, squeezing out moisture as possible.
In a large bowl, combine garlic, red pepper flakes, oregano, Parmesan cheese, bread crumbs, and egg until well-blended. Add the broccoli rice and stir until the dough is well-incorporated. The dough should stick together when it is shaped into a ball.
Press the dough in the center of the prepared baking sheet, forming it into a 12-inches round with a thickness of 1/3-inch. Drizzle with olive oil and season the crust with sea salt.
Let it bake inside the preheated oven, positioning it on the top rack, for about 18-20 minutes until the edges are lightly browned and the edges are crisp.
Nutrition:
Calories: 123
Total Carbohydrate: 9.4 g
Cholesterol: 55 mg
Total Fat: 6.5 g
Protein: 8.4 g
Sodium: 743 mg

Cauliflower Almond Pizza Crust

Preparation Time: 15 minutes
Cooking Time: 45 minutes
Serving: 8

Ingredients:
1 head cauliflower, chopped
1 cup almond flour
3 eggs
1/2 tsp. oregano
1/2 tsp. thyme
1/2 tsp. rosemary
1 dash salt
1 tsp. all-purpose flour

Directions:
Heat oven to 230 degrees C/450 degrees C.
In a blender or food processor, put cauliflower and pulse until it breaks down to the size of rice grains. Place on baking sheet.
Roast in oven for 10 minutes until soft.
Move softened cauliflower in a big bowl. Put in rosemary, thyme, oregano, eggs, and almond flour. Mix well until a ball of dough is formed.
Dust flour on a pizza pan. Place dough on pan using a spatula to create the crust.
Bake crust in oven until edges become crispy and it is golden brown for 20 minutes.
Nutrition:
Calories: 137
Total Carbohydrate: 7.7 g
Cholesterol: 70 mg
Total Fat: 9.7 g
Protein: 7.1 g
Sodium: 96 mg

Cauliflower Pizza Crust

Preparation Time: 15 minutes
Cooking Time: 1 hour
Serving: 6

Ingredients:
1/2 head cauliflower, coarsely chopped
1/2 cup shredded Italian cheese blend
1/4 cup chopped fresh parsley
1 egg
1 tsp. chopped garlic
salt and ground black pepper to taste

Directions:
Put pieces of cauliflower through the food processor's feeding tube with the grating blade. Pulse until all cauliflower got shredded.
In a saucepan, put a steamer insert. Put enough water to reach until the steamer's bottom. Boil. Add cauliflower, steam, cover, for 15 minutes until tender. Move cauliflower to a big bowl and keep in the fridge for 15 minutes until cooled with occasional stirring.

Preheat oven to 230 degrees C or 450 degrees F. line parchment paper or a silicon mat on a baking sheet.

Mix pepper, salt, garlic, egg, parsley, and Italian cheese blend in the cauliflower until well combined. Pour mixture on prepared baking sheet.

Press and form into a pizza crust.

Bake in the preheated oven for 15 minutes until light brown.

Nutrition:
Calories: 59
Total Carbohydrate: 3.3 g
Cholesterol: 38 mg
Total Fat: 3.5 g
Protein: 4.3 g
Sodium: 109

Cauliflower Pizza Crust

Preparation Time: 10 minutes
Cooking Time: 43 minutes
Serving: 4

Ingredients:
1 (12 oz.) package Green Giant® Riced Cauliflower
1 egg
1/3 cup shredded mozzarella cheese
1 tbsp. grated Parmesan cheese
Your favorite pizza toppings

Directions:
Preheat oven to 400 degrees F. Microwave Green Giant Riced Cauliflower by following the package directions. Drain the cooked cauliflower using a colander. Press out as much moisture as you can using paper towels. Mix in cheeses and egg.

Use nonstick cooking spray to spray a baking sheet. Press out the cauliflower mixture to a circle that's 11 inches.

Bake until crust is crisp and edges are brown for 25 minutes.

Top with preferred pizza toppings. Bake for 8-10 minutes.

Nutrition: Calories: 67
Total Carbohydrate: 4.4 g
Cholesterol: 54 mg
Total Fat: 3.1 g Protein: 6.3 g
Sodium: 115 mg

Cheesy Cauliflower Pizza Crust

Preparation Time: 15 minutes
Cooking Time: 59 minutes
Serving: 4

Ingredients:
1 head cauliflower, broken into florets
1 egg
1/2 cup finely shredded mozzarella cheese
1/2 tsp. oregano 1 pinch salt

Directions:
Preheat oven to 200 degrees C or 400 degrees F. Line parchment paper on a baking sheet.
In a food processor, put cauliflower florets and pulse until they are the size of rice grains.
Get a big pot with an inch of water and bring to a boil. Put in cauliflower "rice" and cook for 4-5 minutes until softened. Drain using a fine sieve and cool under running water.
Place cauliflower on a dish towel that's clean. Roll it up and twist the edges. Squeeze as much water as you can.
Move cauliflower to a big bowl. Add salt, oregano, mozzarella cheese, and egg and stir well. Place on a lined baking sheet till it's around half an inch thick.
Bake in the preheated oven for 35 minutes until light golden brown in color and firm to touch.
Nutrition: Calories: 54
Total Carbohydrate: 7.8 g
Cholesterol: 46 mg
Total Fat: 1.4 g Protein: 4.4 g
Sodium: 99 mg

Easy Flatbread With Fresh Herbs

Preparation Time: 15 minutes
Cooking Time: 1 hour 30 minutes
Serving: 8
Ingredients:

1 lb. prepared unbaked pizza dough
1 tsp. all-purpose flour for rolling, or as needed
1 tbsp. extra-virgin olive oil
1 tbsp. chopped fresh thyme
1 tsp. coarse salt, or to taste
Directions:
Roll dough out on a surface that's lightly floured to half an inch in thickness. Move to a baking sheet. Pierce the dough a several times using a fork. Evenly spread olive oil on dough with your hand or a pastry brush. Loosely cover using plastic wrap and let stand for an hour up to overnight.
Preheat oven to 230 degrees C or 450 degrees F. Sprinkle salt and thyme on dough.
Bake in the preheated oven for 15 minutes until golden brown.
Nutrition: Calories: 166 Calories;
Total Carbohydrate: 27.2 g
Cholesterol: 0 mg
Total Fat: 3.7 g Protein: 5 g
Sodium: 669 mg

Cajun Bread In Bread Machine

Preparation Time: 10 minutes
Cooking Time: 2 hours
Servings: 12
Ingredients:
1 tsp of active dry yeast
1 tsp of Cajun seasoning or Creole
1 tbsp of sugar
2 cups of bread flour

Scant 1/2 tsp of salt or 3/4 tsp if your Cajun seasoning does not have salt)
2 tsp of soften butter
2 tsp of finely chopped garlic
1/4 cup of chopped green bell pepper
1/4 cup of chopped onion
1/2 cup of water

Directions:

Combine the ingredients as instructed in your bread machine instruction into the bread machine pan.

Turn to the basic/white bread mode and bake on medium crust or dark color.

Withdraw bread from pan and let cool on a wire rack, slice with a sharp knife into slices.

Note: (Do not use delay cycles for bread)

Nutrition:
Calories: 47 kcal
Fat 2g
Carbohydrates 7g
protein 1g

Chive And Dill Bread

Preparation Time: 10 minutes
Cooking Time: 3 hours
Servings: 1-1/2 pounds (16)

Ingredients:

3/4 cup of water (70° to 80°)
1/2 cup of spreadable cream cheese chive and onion
2 tbsp of sugar
2 tsp of dill weed
1-1/4 tsp of salt
3 cups of all-purpose flour
1 package of yeast (active dry) (1/4 ounce)

Directions:

Combine all the bread ingredients in the bread maker manufacturer's suggested order in your bread machine pan.

Select basic bread setting with medium or light crust and loaf size. Close lid and press start.

Once it is about 5 minutes into the mixing, check and add about 1 to 2 tbsp of water or more flour if needed.

Once done, Remove bread from pan and let cool on wire rack before slicing.

Nutrition:
Calories: 121 kcal
Fat 3g
Carbohydrates 20g
protein 3g

Cajun Sandwich Roll

Preparation Time: 10 minutes
Cooking Time: 2 hours
Servings: 12

Ingredients:

1 tsp of active dry yeast
1 tsp of Cajun seasoning or Creole
1 tbsp of sugar
2 cups of bread flour
Scant 1/2 tsp of salt or 3/4 tsp if your Cajun seasoning does not have salt)
2 tsp of soften butter
2 tsp of finely chopped garlic
1/4 cup of chopped green bell pepper
1/4 cup of chopped onion
1/2 cup of water
1 egg white for brushing
Sesame seeds for sprinkling (optional)
1 tbsp of water for brushing

Directions:
Combine the ingredients in the bucket of your bread machine, push the dough setting.
One the ingredients are properly mixed and knead, remove from the pan and cut into 10 to 12 equal parts and shape each of the dough into rolls.
Lightly grease a large baking sheet or line with parchment paper and transfer the roll onto the baking sheet.
Cover rolls using a damp kitchen towel, allow sitting for about 35 to 45 minutes until rolls rise or it has doubled in size.
In a small bowl, whisk together 1 tablespoon of water and egg white, brush each of the rolls with the mixture. Sprinkle top of rolls with sesame seeds, if using.
Bake for about 15 minutes in a preheated oven at 350 F, or until golden brown.
Nutrition:
Calories: 47 kcal
Fat 2g
Carbohydrates 7g
protein 1g

Rosemary Garlic Bread

Preparation Time: 10 minutes
Cooking Time: 3 hours
Servings: 6
Ingredients:
3 cups of all-purpose flour

2 tsp of crushed dried rosemary
1/2 tsp of garlic powder
1/2 tsp of ground thyme
3 tbsp of olive oil
1 1/2 tsp of salt
3 tbsp of white sugar
2 1/2 tsp of active dry yeast
1 cup of warm water
Direction:
Combine all the bread ingredients in the bread maker manufacturer's suggested order in your bread machine pan. Select the basic setting with medium or light crust and loaf size. Close lid and press start. Once it is about 5 minutes into the mixing, check and add about 1 to 2 tbsp of water or more flour if needed. Once done, Remove bread from pan and let cool on wire rack before slicing.
Nutrition:
Calories: 319 kcal
Fat 7.5g
Carbohydrates 55g
protein 7.2g

Basil Herbed Bread

Preparation Time: 10 minutes
Cooking Time: 3 hours
Servings: 1-1/2 pound
Ingredients:
2-1/4 teaspoons active dry yeast
3-1/2 cups bread flour
1/2 teaspoon dried thyme
3/4 teaspoon dried basil
1-1/2 teaspoons salt
1-1/2 teaspoons sugar

2 tablespoons mashed potato
flakes
2 tablespoons dried minced
onion
1 tablespoon butter, softened
1-1/2 cups water (70° to 80°)

Directions:

Combine all the bread
ingredients in the bread maker
manufacturer's suggested order
in your bread machine pan.
Select the basic setting with
medium or light crust and loaf
size. Close lid and press start.
Once it is about 5 minutes
into the mixing, check and
add about 1 to 2 tbsp of water
or more flour if needed.
Once done, Remove bread
from pan and let cool on wire
rack before slicing.

Nutrition:

Calories: 101 kcal

Fat 1g

Carbohydrates 20g

protein 4g

Olive Cheddar Bread

Preparation Time: 10 minutes
Cooking Time: 3 hours
Servings: 1- 1/2 pounds 16

Ingredients:
3/4 cup of pimiento-stuffed olives, drained thoroughly and sliced
2 tsp of active dry yeast
3 cups of bread flour
1-1/4 cups of shredded sharp cheddar cheese
3/4 tsp of salt
4 tsp of sugar
1 cup of water (70° to 80°)

Directions:
Combine all the bread ingredients in order suggested by manufacturer in the bread machine pan with the exception of olives.
Push basic bread setting and the crust you want with loaf size.
Once it's about 5 minutes into the mixing, check and add about 1 to 2 tablespoons of water or more flour if needed.
Add the olives just 5 minutes before final kneading or at the raisin or nut sound. (Your machine may beep to notify you).
Withdraw bread from pan and let cool on a wire rack, slice with a sharp knife into slices.
Nutrition: Calories: 124 kcal Fat 4g Carbohydrates 18g protein 5g

Bread Machine Argentine Chimichurri

Preparation Time: 5 minutes
Cooking Time: 1 hour 15 minutes
Servings: 15

Ingredients:
2 tsp of active dry yeast
3 cups of bread flour
3 tbsp of wheat bran
1 tbsp of white sugar
1 1/2 tsp of salt
3 tbsp of fresh parsley
3 tbsp of chopped onion
2 cloves garlic, minced
3/4 tsp of dried oregano
1/8 tsp of cayenne pepper
3 tbsp of olive oil
1 1/2 tbsp of white wine vinegar 1 cup water

Directions: Combine all the bread ingredients in the bread maker manufacturer's suggested order in your bread machine pan. Select basic or white bread settings with loaf size and crust color. Close lid and press start.
Once it is about 5 minutes into the mixing, check and add about 1 to 2 tbsp of water or more flour if needed.
Once done, Remove bread from pan and let cool on wire rack before slicing.
Nutrition: Calories: 33 kcal Fat 2.8g Carbohydrates 1.9g protein 0.8g

Herb Bread Machine Bread

Preparation Time: 15 minutes
Cooking Time: 3 hours 40 minutes
Servings: 16

Ingredients:
2-1/4 tsp of active dry yeast
3 cups of bread flour
1/2 tsp of garlic powder
1/2 tsp of dried basil
1/2 tsp of minced garlic
1 tsp of salt
1 tbsp of grated Parmesan cheese
1 tbsp of softened butter
1-1/2 tsp of sugar
1/4 cup of warm sour cream (70° to 80°)
1/4 cup of warm water (70° to 80°)
2/3 cup of warm milk (70° to 80°)

Directions:
1. Place the entire ingredients in bread machine pan in order suggested by manufacturer.
2. Push the basic bread setting and light crust with loaf size.
3. Once it is about 5 minutes into the mixing, check and add about 1 to 2 tablespoons of water or more flour if needed.
4: Once done, remove bread from pan and let cool on wire rack before slicing.
Nutrition:
Calories: 100 kcal
Fat 2g
Carbohydrates 17g
protein 4g

Chili Beer Bread

Preparation Time: 5 minutes
Cooking Time: 3 hours
Servings: 10

Ingredients:
2 tsp of active dry yeast
1/2 tsp of salt
1/4 tsp of garlic powder
1 tsp of chili powder
1 tbsp of dried minced onion
1/8 tsp of ground cumin
2 1/4 cups bread flour
1 tbsp of olive oil
1/4 tsp of hot chile oil
1/4 tsp of ground cayenne pepper
1 tsp of beef bouillon
7/8 cup of beer

Directions:
Combine all the bread ingredients in the bread maker manufacturer's suggested order in your bread machine pan. Select the French bread or White Bread with loaf size. Close lid and press start. Once it is 5 minutes into the mixing, check and add about 1 to 2 tbsp of water or more flour if needed. Once done, Remove bread from pan and let cool on wire rack before slicing.

Nutrition:
Calories: 28 kcal
Fat 1.6g
Carbohydrates 1.7g
protein 0.5g

Oregano Basil Herb Bread

Preparation Time: 10 minutes
Cooking Time: 3 hours
Servings: 8

Ingredients:

2 tsp of bread machine yeast
2 tbsp of all-purpose flour
3 cups of all-purpose flour
1 tsp of dried basil
1 tsp of dried oregano
2 tsp of dried rosemary leaves, crushed
2 tbsp of extra-virgin olive oil
2 tbsp of white sugar
1 tsp of salt
1 egg, beaten
1 cup of warm water

Directions:

Combine all the bread ingredients in the bread maker manufacturer's suggested order in your bread machine pan. Select the basic setting with light crust and loaf size. Close lid and press start.

Once it is about 5 minutes into the mixing, check and add about 1 to 2 tbsp of water or more flour if needed. Once done, Remove bread from pan and let cool on wire rack before slicing.

Nutrition:
Calories: 234 kcal
Fat 4.6g
Carbohydrates 41g
protein 6.3g

Onion And Dill Herb Bread

Preparation Time: 10 minutes
Cooking Time: 3 hours
Servings: 8

Ingredients:

2 tsp of bread machine yeast
2 tbsp of all-purpose flour
3 cups of all-purpose flour
1/4 cup finely chopped onion
1 tablespoon dried dill
2 tbsp of extra-virgin olive oil
2 tbsp of white sugar
1 tsp of salt
1 egg, beaten
1 cup of warm water

Directions:

Combine all the bread ingredients in the bread maker manufacturer's suggested order in your bread machine pan. Select the basic setting with light crust with loaf size. Close lid and press start.

Once it is 5 minutes into the mixing, check and add about 1 to 2 tbsp of water or more flour if needed.

Once done, Remove bread from pan and let cool on wire rack before slicing.

Nutrition:
Calories: 234 kcal
Fat 4.6g
Carbohydrates 41g
protein 6.3g

Classic White Bread I

Preparation Time: 25 minutes
Cooking Time: 25 minutes
Servings: Makes 1 loaf

Ingredients:

16 slice bread (2 pounds)
1½ cups lukewarm water
1 tablespoon + 1 teaspoon olive oil
1½ teaspoons sugar
1 teaspoon table salt
¼ teaspoon baking soda
2½ cups all-purpose flour
1 cup white bread flour
2½ teaspoons bread machine yeast

12 slice bread (1½ pounds)
1 cups lukewarm water
¾ tablespoon + 1 teaspoon olive oil
1⅛ teaspoons sugar
¾ teaspoon table salt
⅛ teaspoon baking soda
1½ cups all-purpose flour
¾ cup white bread flour
1½ teaspoons bread machine yeast

Directions:

Choose the size of loaf you would like to make and measure your ingredients. Add the ingredients to the bread pan in the order listed above.

Place the pan in the bread machine and close the lid. Turn on the bread maker. Select the White/Basic setting, then the loaf size, and finally the crust color. Start the cycle. When the cycle is finished and the bread is baked, carefully remove the pan from the machine. Use a pot holder as the handle will be very hot. Let rest for a few minutes.

Remove the bread from the pan and allow to cool on a

wire rack for at least 10 minutes before slicing.
Nutrition:
Calories 124
fat 4.9 g
carbs 17.2 g
sodium178 mg
protein 2 g

Classic White Bread II

Preparation Time: 25 minutes
Cooking Time: 25 minutes
Servings: Makes 1 loaf
Ingredients:
16 slice bread (2 pounds)
1 1/2 cups water, lukewarm between 80 and 90ºF
3 tablespoons unsalted butter, melted
1 tablespoon sugar
3 tablespoons dry milk powder
1 1/4 teaspoons table salt
4 cup white bread flour
1 1/2 teaspoons bread machine yeast
12 slice bread (1 ½ pounds)
1 1/4 cups water, lukewarm between 80 and 90ºF
2 tablespoons unsalted butter, melted
2 teaspoons sugar
2 tablespoons dry milk powder
1 teaspoons table salt
3 1/4 cup white bread flour
1 1/4 teaspoons bread machine yeast
Directions:
Choose the size of loaf you would like to make and measure your ingredients.

Add the ingredients to the bread pan in the order listed above.
Place the pan in the bread machine and close the lid. Turn on the bread maker. Select the White/Basic setting, then the loaf size, and finally the crust color. Start the cycle. When the cycle is finished and the bread is baked, carefully remove the pan from the machine. Use a pot holder as the handle will be very hot. Let rest for a few minutes. Remove the bread from the pan and allow to cool on a wire rack for at least 10 minutes before slicing.
Nutrition:
Calories 148
fat 3.6 g
carbs 23.4 g
sodium197 mg
protein 3.4 g

Classic White Sandwich Bread

Preparation Time: 25 minutes
Cooking Time: 25 minutes
Servings: Makes 1 loaf
Ingredients:
16 slice bread (2 pounds)
1 cup water, lukewarm between 80 and 90ºF
2 tablespoons unsalted butter, melted
1 teaspoon table salt
1/4 cup sugar
2 egg whites or 1 egg, beaten
3 cups white bread flour
1 1/2 teaspoons bread machine yeast

12 slice bread (1 ½ pounds)
3/4 cup water, lukewarm
between 80 and 90ºF
1 1/2 tablespoons unsalted
butter, melted
3/4 teaspoon table salt
1 ½ ounces sugar
2 egg whites or 1 egg, beaten
2 1/4 cups white bread flour
1 1/8 teaspoons bread
machine yeast

Directions:

Choose the size of loaf you
would like to make and
measure your ingredients.
Add the ingredients to the
bread pan in the order listed
above.
Place the pan in the bread
machine and close the lid.
Turn on the bread maker.
Select the White/Basic setting,
then the loaf size, and finally
the crust color. Start the cycle.
When the cycle is finished and
the bread is baked, carefully
remove the pan from the
machine. Use a pot holder as
the handle will be very hot. Let
rest for a few minutes.
Remove the bread from the
pan and allow to cool on a
wire rack for at least 10
minutes before slicing.
Nutrition:
Calories 126
fat 2.3 g
carbs 23 g
sodium137 mg
protein 4 g

Almond Milk Bread

Preparation Time: 30 minutes

Cooking Time: 30 minutes
Servings: Makes 1 loaf
Ingredients:
16 slice bread (2 pounds)
1 cup lukewarm milk
2 eggs, at room temperature
2⅔ tablespoons butter, melted
and cooled
⅓ cup sugar
1 teaspoon table salt
2⅓ teaspoons lemon zest
4 cups white bread flour
2¼ teaspoons bread machine
yeast
½ cup slivered almonds,
chopped
½ cup golden raisins, chopped
12 slice bread (1½ pounds)
¾ cup lukewarm milk
2 eggs, at room temperature
2 tablespoons butter, melted
and cooled
¼ cup sugar
1 teaspoon table salt
2 teaspoons lemon zest
3 cups white bread flour
2 teaspoons bread machine
yeast
⅓ cup slivered almonds,
chopped
⅓ cup golden raisins, chopped
Directions:
Choose the size of loaf you
would like to make and
measure your ingredients.
Add all of the ingredients
except for the raisins and
almonds to the bread pan in
the order listed above.
Place the pan in the bread
machine and close the lid.
Turn on the bread maker.
Select the White/Basic or

Fruit/Nut (if your machine has this setting) setting, then the loaf size, and finally the crust color. Start the cycle. When the machine signals to add ingredients, add the raisins and almonds. (Some machines have a fruit/nut hopper where you can add the raisins and almonds when you start the machine. The machine will automatically add them to the dough during the baking process.)

When the cycle is finished and the bread is baked, carefully remove the pan from the machine. Use a pot holder as the handle will be very hot. Let rest for a few minutes.

Remove the bread from the pan and allow to cool on a wire rack for at least 10 minutes before slicing.

Nutrition:
Calories 193
fat 4.6 g
carbs 29.4 g
sodium214 mg
protein 5.7 g

Hazelnut Honey Bread

Preparation Time: 30 minutes
Cooking Time: 30 minutes
Servings: Makes 1 loaf

Ingredients:
16 slice bread (2 pounds)
1⅓ cups lukewarm milk
2 eggs, at room temperature
5 tablespoons unsalted butter, melted
¼ cup honey
1 teaspoon pure vanilla extract
1 teaspoon table salt
4 cups white bread flour
1 cup toasted hazelnuts, finely ground
2 teaspoons bread machine yeast
12 slice bread (1½ pounds)
1 cup lukewarm milk
1 egg, at room temperature
3¾ tablespoons unsalted butter, melted
3 tablespoons honey
¾ teaspoon pure vanilla extract
¾ teaspoon table salt
3 cups white bread flour
¾ cup toasted hazelnuts, finely ground
1½ teaspoons bread machine yeast

Directions:
Choose the size of loaf you would like to make and measure your ingredients.

Add the ingredients to the bread pan in the order listed above.

Place the pan in the bread machine and close the lid. Turn on the bread maker. Select the White/Basic setting, then the loaf size, and finally the crust color. Start the cycle.

When the cycle is finished and the bread is baked, carefully remove the pan from the machine. Use a pot holder as the handle will be very hot. Let rest for a few minutes.

Remove the bread from the pan and allow to cool on a wire rack for at least 10 minutes before slicing.

Nutrition:
Calories 211
fat 7.6 g
carbs 28.7 g
sodium153 mg
protein 4.3 g

Pistachio Cherry Bread

Preparation Time: 30 minutes
Cooking Time: 30 minutes
Servings: Makes 1 loaf
Ingredients:
16 slice bread (2 pounds)
1⅛ cups lukewarm water
1 egg, at room temperature
¼ cup butter, softened
¼ cup packed dark brown sugar
1½ teaspoons table salt
3¾ cups white bread flour
½ teaspoon ground nutmeg
Dash allspice
2 teaspoons bread machine yeast
1 cup dried cherries
½ cup unsalted pistachios, chopped
12 slice bread (1½ pounds)
¾ cup lukewarm water
1 egg, at room temperature
3 tablespoons butter, softened
3 tablespoons packed dark brown sugar
1⅛ teaspoons table salt
2¾ cups white bread flour
½ teaspoon ground nutmeg
Dash allspice
1½ teaspoons bread machine yeast
¾ cup dried cherries

⅓ cup unsalted pistachios, chopped
Directions:
Choose the size of loaf you would like to make and measure your ingredients. Add all of the ingredients except for the pistachios and cherries to the bread pan in the order listed above.
Place the pan in the bread machine and close the lid. Turn on the bread maker. Select the White/Basic or Fruit/Nut (if your machine has this setting) setting, then the loaf size, and finally the crust color. Start the cycle. When the machine signals to add ingredients, add the pistachios and cherries. (Some machines have a fruit/nut hopper where you can add the pistachios and cherries when you start the machine. The machine will automatically add them to the dough during the baking process.)
When the cycle is finished and the bread is baked, carefully remove the pan from the machine. Use a pot holder as the handle will be very hot. Let rest for a few minutes. Remove the bread from the pan and allow to cool on a wire rack for at least 10 minutes before slicing.
Nutrition:
Calories 196
fat 5.3 g
carbs 27.8 g
sodium237 mg
protein 4.4 g

Super Spice Bread

Preparation Time: 25-30 minutes
Cooking Time: 25-30 minutes
Servings: Makes 1 loaf

Ingredients:
16 slice bread (2 pounds)
1⅓ cups lukewarm milk
2 eggs, at room temperature
2 tablespoons unsalted butter, melted
2⅔ tablespoons honey
1⅓ teaspoons table salt
4 cups white bread flour
1⅓ teaspoons ground cinnamon
⅔ teaspoon ground cardamom
⅔ teaspoon ground nutmeg
2¼ teaspoons bread machine yeast
12 slice bread (1½ pounds)
1 cup lukewarm milk
2 eggs, at room temperature
1½ tablespoons unsalted butter, melted
2 tablespoons honey
1 teaspoon table salt
3 cups white bread flour
1 teaspoon ground cinnamon
½ teaspoon ground cardamom
½ teaspoon ground nutmeg
2 teaspoons bread machine yeast

Directions:
Choose the size of loaf you would like to make and measure your ingredients.
Add the ingredients to the bread pan in the order listed above.
Place the pan in the bread machine and close the lid.
Turn on the bread maker. Select the White/Basic setting, then the loaf size, and finally the crust color. Start the cycle. When the cycle is finished and the bread is baked, carefully remove the pan from the machine. Use a pot holder as the handle will be very hot. Let rest for a few minutes. Remove the bread from the pan and allow to cool on a wire rack for at least 10 minutes before slicing.

Nutrition:
Calories 163
fat 2.8 g
carbs 27.6 g
sodium 197 mg
protein 4.8 g

Cinnamon Milk Bread

Preparation Time: 25-30 minutes
Cooking Time: 25-30 minutes
Servings: Makes 1 loaf

Ingredients:
16 slice bread (2 pounds)
1⅔ cups lukewarm milk
1 egg, at room temperature
⅓ cup unsalted butter, melted

⅔ cup sugar
⅔ teaspoon table salt
4 cups white bread flour
2 teaspoons ground cinnamon
2¼ teaspoons bread machine yeast
12 slice bread (1½ pounds)
1 cup lukewarm milk
1 egg, at room temperature
¼ cup unsalted butter, melted
½ cup sugar
½ teaspoon table salt
3 cups white bread flour
1½ teaspoons ground cinnamon
2 teaspoons bread machine yeast

Directions:
Choose the size of loaf you would like to make and measure your ingredients. Add the ingredients to the bread pan in the order listed above.
Place the pan in the bread machine and close the lid. Turn on the bread maker. Select the White/Basic setting, then the loaf size, and finally the crust color. Start the cycle. When the cycle is finished and the bread is baked, carefully remove the pan from the machine. Use a pot holder as the handle will be very hot. Let rest for a few minutes. Remove the bread from the pan and allow to cool on a wire rack for at least 10 minutes before slicing.
Nutrition:
Calories 187
fat 5.1 g
carbs 33.4 g

sodium143 mg
protein 4.6 g

Cardamom Honey Bread
Preparation Time: 25-30 minutes
Cooking Time: 25-30 minutes
Servings: Makes 1 loaf
Ingredients:
16 slice bread (2 pounds)
1⅛ cups lukewarm milk
1 egg, at room temperature
2 teaspoons unsalted butter, melted
¼ cup honey
1⅓ teaspoons table salt
4 cups white bread flour
1⅓ teaspoons ground cardamom
1⅔ teaspoons bread machine yeast
12 slice bread (1½ pounds)
¾ cup lukewarm milk
1 egg, at room temperature

1½ teaspoons unsalted butter, melted
3 tablespoons honey
1 teaspoon table salt
3 cups white bread flour
1 teaspoon ground cardamom
1¼ teaspoons bread machine yeast

Directions:

Choose the size of loaf you would like to make and measure your ingredients. Add the ingredients to the bread pan in the order listed above.

Place the pan in the bread machine and close the lid. Turn on the bread maker. Select the White/Basic setting, then the loaf size, and finally the crust color. Start the cycle. When the cycle is finished and the bread is baked, carefully remove the pan from the machine. Use a pot holder as the handle will be very hot. Let rest for a few minutes.

Remove the bread from the pan and allow to cool on a wire rack for at least 10 minutes before slicing.

Nutrition:
Calories 148
fat 2.2 g
carbs 28.2 g
sodium212 mg
protein 4.8 g

Double Cheese Overload

Preparation Time: 30-45 minutes

Cooking Time: 30-45 minutes
Servings: Makes 1 loaf
Ingredients: 80 degrees F
¾ cup + 1 tablespoons milk at
2 teaspoons butter, melted and cooled
4 teaspoons sugar
2/3 teaspoon salt
1/3 teaspoon fresh ground pepper
Pinch of cayenne pepper
1 cup (4 ounces) shredded aged sharp cheddar cheese
1/3 cup shredded/grated parmesan cheese
2 cups white bread flour
¾ teaspoon instant yeast

Directions: Add all of the ingredients to your bread machine, carefully following the instructions of the manufacturer. Set the program of your bread machine to Basic/White Bread and set crust type to Light.

Press START. Wait until the cycle completes. Once the loaf is ready, take the bucket out and let the loaf cool for 5 minutes.

Gently shake the bucket to remove the loaf. Transfer to a cooling rack, slice, and serve. Enjoy!

Nutrition: Total Carbs: 28g,
Fiber: 1g
protein: 9g
fat: 4g,
Calories: 183

Blue Cheese & Onion Loaf

Preparation Time: 30 minutes

Cooking Time: 30 minutes
Servings: Makes 1 loaf

Ingredients:

¾ cup + 1 tablespoon water at
80 degrees F
1 whole egg
2 teaspoons melted butter,
cooled
3 tablespoons powdered skim
milk
2 teaspoons sugar
½ teaspoon salt
1/3 cup crumbled blue cheese
2 teaspoons dried onion flakes
2 cups white bread flour
3 tablespoons instantly
mashed potato flakes
¾ teaspoons bread machine/
active dry yeast

Directions:

Add all of the ingredients to
your bread machine, carefully
following the instructions of
the manufacturer.
Set the program of your bread
machine to Basic/White Bread
and set crust type to Light.
Press START.
Wait until the cycle completes.
Once the loaf is ready, take the
bucket out and let the loaf
cool for 5 minutes.
Gently shake the bucket to
remove the loaf.
Transfer to a cooling rack,
slice, and serve.
Enjoy!
Nutrition: Total Carbs: 27g,
Fiber: 1g
protein: 6g
fat: 3g,
Calories: 164

Garlic Cheese Bread Loaf

Preparation Time:1 0 minutes
Cooking Time: 45 minutes
Servings: 10

Ingredients:

1 Tbsp. parsley, chopped
½ cup butter, unsalted and
softened
2 Tbsp. garlic powder
6 large eggs
½ tsp. oregano seasoning
1 tsp. baking powder
2 cups almond flour
½ tsp. xanthan gum
1 cup cheddar cheese,
shredded
½ tsp. salt

Directions:

Preheat the oven to 355F.
Line a baking pan with
parchment paper.
In a food blender, pulse the
eggs until smooth. Then
combine the butter and pulse
for 1 minute more.
Blend the almond flour and
baking powder for 90 seconds
or until thickens.
Finally, combine the garlic,
oregano, parsley, and cheese
until mixed.
Pour into the prepared and
bake in the oven for 45
minutes.
Cool, slice, and serve.
Nutrition:
Calories: 299
fat: 27g, Carb: 4g
protein: 11g

Amazing Whole Wheat Pizza Crust

Preparation Time: 25 minutes
Cooking Time: 2 hours
Servings: 10

Ingredients:

1 tsp. white sugar
1 1/2 cups warm water (110 degrees F/45 degrees C)
1 tbsp. active dry yeast
1 tbsp. olive oil
1 tsp. salt
2 cups whole wheat flour
1 1/2 cups all-purpose flour

Directions: Melt sugar in a big bowl with warm water. Sprinkle yeast on top and let stand for 10 minutes until foamy. Mix in salt and olive oil in the yeast mixture. Mix in a cup of all-purpose flour and the whole wheat flour until a dough starts to come together. Tip dough on a surface floured with leftover all-purpose flour. Knead until the flour gets absorbed for 10 minutes and the dough ball is smooth. Put dough in a bowl that's been oiled and turn it to coat the dough's surface. Loosely cover using a towel and let it stand for an hour in a warm area until it doubles in size. When the dough doubles, tip it out on a surface that's lightly floured. Halve it to create 2 thin crust or leave it whole to create 1 thick crust. Shape to a tight ball. Let rise for 45 minutes until it doubles. Preheat oven to 220 degrees C or 425 degrees F.

Roll the dough ball using a rolling pin until it can't stretch anymore. Drape in over both of your fists and pull the edges outwards gently as you rotate the crust. When you reach your desired circle size, put on a pizza pan that's well-oiled. Top it with your preferred toppings such as sauce, cheese, meat or vegetables
Bake for 16-20 minutes, depending on the thickness, in the preheated oven, until the edges are golden and the crust becomes crisp while the cheese melted on top.

Nutrition: Calories: 167 Calories
Total Carbohydrate: 32.6 g
Cholesterol: 0 mg
Total Fat: 2 g
protein: 5.7 g
Sodium: 236 mg

Bread Machine Pizza Dough

Preparation Time: 10 minutes
Cooking Time: 2 hours
Servings: 6
Ingredients: 1 cup flat beer
2 tbsps. Butter 2 tbsps. sugar
1 tsp. salt
2 1/2 cups all-purpose flour
2 1/4 tsps. Yeast

Directions: In the bread machine, put in the beer, butter, sugar, salt, flour and yeast following the order of ingredients suggested by the manufacturer. Choose the Dough setting on the machine and press the Start button. Once the machine has finished the whole cycle, take the dough out from the bread machine. Roll it out or flatten it to fit into the prepared pizza pan. Use a brush to coat the dough with a little bit of olive oil. Cover the dough and let it sit for 15 minutes. Preheat the oven to 400°F (200°C).
Scatter the sauce and the toppings evenly over the dough. Put in the preheated oven and bake for about 24 minutes until the crust is crispy on the exterior and is slightly brown in color.
Nutrition:
Calories: 262
Calories
Total Carbohydrate: 46 g,
Cholesterol: 10 mg, Total Fat: 4.4 g
protein: 6.2 g, Sodium: 418 mg

Bread Machine Thin Crust Pizza Dough

Preparation Time: 1 hour 10 minutes
Cooking Time: 1 hour 15 minutes
Servings: 8
Ingredients:
3/4 cup warm water - 100 to 110 degrees F (40 to 45 degrees C)
2 cups all-purpose flour
1/2 tsp. salt
1/4 tsp. white sugar
1 tsp. active dry yeast
2 tsps. olive oil

Directions:
Put warm water in the bread machine's pan then add flour over the water. Sprinkle sugar and salt then top with yeast. Put machine on dough setting and select start. When the machine finishes the dough, move to a surface that's well-floured.
Preheat oven to 220 degrees C or 425 degrees F
Stretch or roll dough to a thin crust that's around 14 inches across. Allow the dough to be thick at the edges. Put dough on a pizza baking sheet that's 14 inches and brush olive oil on the dough.
Baking in the preheated oven for 5 minutes before removing to top with favorite ingredients, for final baking process.
Nutrition:
Calories: 126
Calories

119

Total Carbohydrate: 24.2 g,
Cholesterol: 0 mg, Total Fat:
1.5 g
protein: 3.4 g, Sodium: 147 mg

Cheesy Pesto Bread

Preparation Time: 20 minutes
Cooking Time: 1 hour
Serving: 12

Ingredients:
2 cups blanched almond flour
½ cup arrowroot powder
½ teaspoon white pepper
2 eggs
¼ cup prepared pesto
1/3 cup Parmesan cheese,
shredded and divided
7 tablespoons flaxseeds meal
½ teaspoon baking soda
Salt, to taste
1 cup full-fat coconut milk
1¾ cups Cheddar cheese,
shredded

Directions
Preheat the oven to 350
degrees F. Line a loaf pan with
lightly, greased parchment
paper.
In a large bowl, place the
almond flour, flax seeds meal,
arrowroot powder, baking
soda, white pepper and salt
and mix well. In another bowl,
add eggs and coconut milk
and beat until well blended.
Add pesto, Cheddar cheese
and ¼ cup of Parmesan cheese
and mix until well blended.
Place the mixture into the
prepared loaf pan and sprinkle
with remaining Parmesan
cheese.

Bake for about 50-60 minutes
or until a skewer inserted in
the center of loaf comes out
clean.
Remove from the oven and
place the pan onto a wire rack
to cool for about 10 minutes.
Carefully invert onto a wire
rack to cool slightly. With a
knife, cut the bread into
desired-sized slices and serve
warm.
Nutrition:
Calories: 306
Total Fat : 24.1g
Saturated Fat: 9g
Protein: 11.9g
Carbs: 12.5g
fiber: 3.5g
Sugar: 1.5g

Cornbread

Preparation time: 15 minutes
Cooking time: 23 minutes
Serving: 12

Ingredients:
1 cup yellow cornmeal
¼ cup white sugar
½ teaspoon baking soda
2 large eggs
¼ cup honey
1 cup all-purpose flour
1 teaspoon baking powder
¼ teaspoon salt
1 cup buttermilk
½ cup butter, melted and
cooled slightly

Directions
Preheat oven to 400 degrees F.
Place a 9-inch square baking
pan in the oven to heat up.

In a large bowl, mix together cornmeal, flour, brown sugar, baking powder, baking soda and salt. With a wooden spoon, create a well in the middle of flour mixture. Add eggs, buttermilk and honey and mix until well blended. Add butter and mix until just blended.

Carefully, place the mixture into heated pan evenly.

Bake for about 20-23 minutes or until a skewer inserted in the center of loaf comes out clean.

Remove from the oven and place onto wire rack to cool for about 10 minutes before serving. Cut into desired-sized pieces and serve.

Nutrition:
Calories: 200
Total Fat: 9.2g
Saturated Fat: 5.3g
Protein: 3.7g
Carbs: 27g
fiber: 1g
Sugar: 11.1g

Nuts & Seeds Bread

Preparation time: 20 minutes
Cooking time: 35 minutes
Serving: 12

Ingredients:

1½ cups blanched almond flour
¼ cup brown flax meal
Salt, to taste
3 tablespoons agave nectar
¾ cup arrowroot powder
½ teaspoon baking soda
4 large eggs
1 teaspoon apple cider vinegar
1/3 cup sunflower seeds
1/3 cup pumpkin seeds
½ cup unsalted pistachios, chopped
¼ cup hazelnuts, chopped
¼ cup walnuts, chopped

Directions:

Preheat oven to 350 degrees F. Line a loaf pan with a lightly, greased parchment paper.

In a large bowl, add almond flour, arrowroot powder, flax meal, baking soda and salt and mix well. In another bowl, add eggs, agave nectar and vinegar and beat until well blended. Add egg mixture into the bowl of flour mixture and mix until well blended. Gently, fold in seeds and nuts.

Transfer the mixture into the prepared loaf pan.

Bake for about 30-35 minutes or until a skewer inserted in the center of loaf comes out clean.

Remove from the oven and place the pan onto a wire rack to cool for about 10 minutes.

Carefully invert the loaf on wire rack to cool completely before slicing. Cut the bread into desired-sized slices and serve.

Nutrition:
Calories: 143
Total Fat: 8.6g
Saturated Fat: 1.2g
Protein: 5.2g
Carbs: 12.4g
fiber: 1.5g
Sugar: 1.8g

Bacon & Jalapeño Bread

Preparation time: 20 minutes
Cooking time: 55 minutes
Serving: 8

Ingredients:
4 ounces thick bacon slices
½ cup coconut flour
Salt, to taste
½ cup coconut oil, melted and cooled
3 large jalapeño peppers, sliced
¼ teaspoon baking soda
6 large eggs
¼ cup water

Directions:
Preheat the oven to 400 degrees F. Grease a baking sheet.

Place bacon and jalapeño peppers onto the prepared baking sheet in a single layer. Bake for about 5 minutes per side.

Remove from the oven and set aside to cool slightly.

Now, preheat the oven to 375 degrees F and lightly, grease a baking dish.

In a food processor, add bacon and jalapeño and pulse until chopped roughly.

In a large bowl, place the coconut flour, baking soda and salt and mix well. In another bowl, add eggs and oil and beat until well blended. Add egg mixture into the bowl of flour mixture and mix until well blended. Gently, fold in bacon mixture.

Place the mixture into the prepared baking dish.

Bake for about 40-45 minutes or until a skewer inserted in the center of bread comes out clean.

Remove from the oven and place the baking dish onto a wire rack to cool for about 10 minutes. Carefully invert the bread onto a wire rack to cool slightly. With a knife, cut the bread into desired-sized slices and serve warm.

Nutrition:
Calories: 254
Total Fat: 23.5g
Saturated Fat: 15g
Protein: 10.2g
Carbs: 1.4g
fiber: 0.5g
Sugar: 0.5g

Zesty Cranberry Bread

Preparation time: 20 minutes
Cooking time: 50 minutes
Serving: 12

Ingredients:
2 cups all-purpose flour
½ teaspoon baking soda

1 egg
1½ teaspoon baking powder
Salt, to taste
¾ cup white sugar
2 tablespoons vegetable oil
¾ cup fresh orange juice
1 cup fresh cranberries,
chopped
½ cup walnuts, chopped
1 tablespoon fresh orange zest,
grated

Directions:
Preheat the oven to 350
degrees F. Grease a 13x9-inch
bread pan.
In a large bowl, place the
flour, baking powder, baking
soda and salt and mix well. In
another bowl, add egg, sugar,
oil and orange juice and beat
until well blended. Add egg
mixture into the bowl of flour
mixture and mix until just
blended. Fold in cranberries,
walnuts and orange zest.
Place the mixture in prepared
loaf pan evenly.
Bake for about 50 minutes or
until a skewer inserted in the
center of loaf comes out clean
Remove from the oven and
transfer onto a wire rack to
cool for about 10 minutes.
Carefully invert the loaf onto
the wire rack to cool
completely before slicing. Cut
the bread loaf into desired-
sized slices and serve.
Nutrition:
Calories: 193
Total Fat: 15.9g
Saturated Fat: 0.8g
Protein: 4g
Carbs: 31.8g

fiber: 1.3g
Sugar: 14.3g

Cheesy Pepperoni Bread

Preparation time: 20 minutes
Cooking time: 50 minutes
Serving: 12

Ingredients:

1¼ cups milk
3 cups all-purpose flour
1 (¼-ounce) package active dry yeast
½ teaspoon garlic powder
1½ tablespoons butter
1 tablespoon sugar
½ teaspoon Italian seasoning
Salt, to taste
8 ounces turkey pepperoni, sliced
Nonstick cooking spray
¼ cup mozzarella cheese, shredded

Directions:

In a small pan, add milk and butter over medium heat and cook until its temperature reaches to 120 degrees F.
In a large bowl, mix together 1½ cups of flour, sugar, yeast, Italian seasoning, garlic powder and salt. Add pepperoni and stir to combine. Add milk mixture and knead for about 3 minutes. Add remaining flour, ½ cup at a time and knead until a sticky dough forms.
Now, place the dough into a well-greased bowl and spray the top with cooking spray evenly. With a plastic wrap, cover the bowl and set aside in warm place for about 1 hour. With your hands, punch the dough down and set aside for about 10 minutes. Place the dough into a greased 8x5-inch loaf pan. With a plastic wrap, cover the loaf pan and set aside in a warm place for about 45 minutes.
Preheat the oven to 375 degrees F.
Bake for about 10 minutes. Now, set the temperature of the oven to 350 degrees F. Bake for about 20-25 minutes. Remove from the oven and sprinkle the cheese on top of bread evenly. Bake for about 10 minutes more.
Remove from the oven and place the pan onto a wire rack to cool for about 10 minutes. Carefully invert the bread onto the wire rack to cool for about 10-15 minutes. With a knife, cut the bread into desired-sized slices and serve.

Nutrition:

Calories: 191
Total Fat : 5g
Saturated Fat: 2.3g
Protein: 10.2g
Carbs: 26.5g
fiber: 1g
Sugar: 2.3g

Chocolaty Banana Bread

Preparation time: 15 minutes
Cooking time: 40 minutes
Serving: 12

Ingredients:
½ cup coconut flour
1 teaspoon baking soda
Pinch of salt
¼ cup coconut oil, melted
1 teaspoon baking powder
½ teaspoon ground cinnamon
½ cup almond butter
1 tablespoon maple syrup
1 teaspoon vanilla extract
2½ cups bananas, peeled and mashed
6 ounces dark chocolate chips

Directions:
Preheat the oven to 350 degrees F. Grease a 9x5-inch loaf pan.
In a large bowl, place the flour, baking powder, baking soda, cinnamon and salt and mix. In another bowl, add egg, almond butter, coconut oil, maple syrup and vanilla extract and beat until well blended. Add bananas and beat well. Add the egg mixture into the bowl of the flour mixture and mix until well blended. Gently, fold in chocolate chips.
Transfer the mixture into prepared loaf pan evenly.
Bake for about 40 minutes or until a skewer inserted in the center of loaf comes out clean. Remove from the oven and place the loaf pan onto a wire rack to cool for about 10 minutes. Carefully invert the loaf onto wire rack to cool completely before slicing. With a sharp knife, cut the loaf into desired-sized slices and serve.
Nutrition:
Calories: 125
Total Fat: 7.6g
Saturated Fat: 5.5g
Protein: 1.3g
Carbs: 15.9g
fiber: 1g
Sugar: 10.7g

Pumpkin Bread

Preparation time: 15 minutes
Cooking time: 1 hour
Serving: 24
Ingredients:
3½ cups all-purpose flour
½ teaspoon baking powder
1 teaspoon ground cloves
1 teaspoon ground allspice
2 teaspoons baking soda
2 teaspoons ground ginger
1 teaspoon ground cinnamon
1 teaspoon salt
4 eggs, beaten
3 cups sugar
2/3 cup water
1 cup canola oil
1 (15-ounce) can pumpkin puree
Directions:
Preheat oven to 350 degrees F. Generously, grease 2 (9x5-inch) loaf pans.
In a large bowl, place the flour, baking soda, baking powder, spices and salt and mix. In another bowl, add eggs, sugar, oil and water and beat until well blended. Add pumpkin puree and beat until well blended. Add egg mixture into the bowl of flour mixture and mix until just blended. Divide the mixture in both prepared loaf pans evenly. Bake for about 1 hour or until a skewer inserted in the center of loaf comes out clean. Remove from the oven and place the pans onto wire racks to cool for about 10 minutes. Carefully invert the loaf onto wire rack to cool completely before slicing. With a sharp knife, cut the loaf into desired-sized slices and serve.
Nutrition:
Calories: 258
Total Fat: 10.1g
Saturated Fat: 1g
Protein: 3g
Carbs: 40.8g
fiber: 1.1g
Sugar: 25.7g

Coconut, Carrot & Zucchini Bread

Preparation time: 20 minutes
Cooking time: 1½ hours
Serving: 12
Ingredients:
2 cups all-purpose flour
½ teaspoon baking powder
2 large eggs, beaten
½ cup granulated sugar
½ teaspoon baking soda
¾ teaspoon salt
¾ cup light brown sugar
½ cup canola oil
1 cup zucchini, grated
1 cup carrots, grated
1¼ cups sweetened coconut, shredded and divided
Directions:
Preheat oven to 375 degrees F. Grease an 8x4-inch loaf pan. In a bowl, add flour, baking soda, baking powder and salt and mix well. In another large bowl, add eggs, sugars and canola oil and beat until smooth. Add zucchini, carrots and ¾ cup of coconut and stir to combine. Add flour mixture and mix until just blended.

Place the mixture into prepared loaf pan evenly and top with remaining coconut. With a piece of foil, cover the loaf pan loosely.

Bake for about 1½ hours or until a skewer inserted in the center of loaf comes out clean. Remove from the oven and place the pan onto a wire rack to cool for about 30 minutes. Carefully invert the loaf onto wire rack to cool completely before slicing. With a sharp knife, cut the loaf into desired-sized slices and serve.

Nutrition:
Calories: 269
Total Fat: 12.9g
Saturated Fat: 3.4g
Protein: 3.7g
Carbs: 35.8g
fiber: 1.6g
Sugar: 18.4g

Beer Bread

Preparation time: 10 minutes
Cooking time: 1 hour
Serving: 12

Ingredients:
3 cups self-rising flour
1 (12 fluid ounces) bottle beer
3 tablespoons white sugar

Directions:
Preheat the oven to 350 degrees F. Grease a 9x5-inch loaf pan.

In a large bowl, add the flour and sugar and mix. Add beer and mix until sticky dough forms.

Place the mixture into prepared pan evenly.

Bake for about 50-60 minutes or until top becomes crunchy. Remove from the oven and place the pan onto a wire rack to cool for about 15 minutes. Carefully invert the loaf onto wire rack to cool completely before slicing. With a sharp knife, cut the loaf into desired-sized slices and serve.

Nutrition:
Calories: 137
Total Fat: 0.1g
Saturated Fat: 0g
Protein: 3.4g
Carbs: 27.9g
fiber: 0.8g
Sugar: 3.1g

Sandwich Bread

Preparation time: 20 minutes
Cooking time: 45 minutes
Serving: 32

Ingredients:
1 (¼-ounce) package active dry yeast
6¼-6¾ cups all-purpose flour
1 tablespoon salt
2¼ cups warm water
3 tablespoons sugar
2 tablespoons canola oil

Directions:
In a large bowl, place yeast and warm water and mix until dissolved. Add 3 cups flour, sugar, salt and oil and beat until well blended and smooth. Slowly, add remaining flour, ½ cup at a time and mix until a soft dough forms.

Transfer the dough onto a generously floured surface and

with your hands, knead until smooth and elastic. Transfer the dough into a greased bowl and turn to coat well. With a plastic wrap, cover the bowl and set aside in a warm place for about 1½ hours.

Uncover and with your hands, punch down the dough. Transfer the dough onto a lightly floured surface and cut into 2 equal sized portions. Shape each dough portion into a loaf. Put 1 loaf into each of a greased 9x5-inch loaf pan. With a plastic wrap, cover the loaf pans and set aside in a warm place for about 30-45 minutes.

Preheat the oven to 375 degrees F.

Bake for about 30-35 minutes or until the top of loaves become golden brown.

Remove from the oven and place onto wire racks to cool for about 8-10 minutes.

Carefully invert the loaves onto wire racks to cool completely before slicing.

With a sharp knife, cut the bread loaves into desired-sized slices and serve.

Nutrition:

Calories: 124

Total Fat: 1.3g

Saturated Fat: 0.1g

Protein: 24.4g

Carbs: 24.4g

fiber: 0.9g

Sugar: 1.4g

Sweet Bread

Preparation Time: 10 minutes
Cooking Time: 3 hours 15 minutes
Servings: 16
Ingredients:
EGG WASH:
Italian seasoning (optional)
1 tbsp of water
1 large egg
Bread
2 tsp of active dry yeast
3 cups of all-purpose flour
1 tsp of salt
1/4 cup of sugar
2 tbsp of softened butter
1 large egg, lightly beaten
1 cup of warm 2% milk (70° to 80°)

Directions:
Combine all the bread ingredients in order suggested by manufacturer in the bread machine pan. Push dough setting.
Once it's about 5 minutes into the mixing, check and add about 1 to 2 tablespoons of water or more flour if needed.
Transfer dough on a floured flat surface and divide in half. Mold each half into ball and press down to slightly flatten. Grease two 9-in round baking sheets, place dough onto the pan and cover for about 45 minutes until rolls rise or it has doubled in size.
In a small bowl, whisk together 1 tablespoon of water and the egg white and brush each of the dough with the mixture.

Sprinkle top of with Italian seasoning, if using.
Bake for about 20-25 minutes in a preheated oven at 350 F. Withdraw bread from pan and let cool on a wire rack.
Nutrition:
Calories: 87 kcal
Fat 2g
Carbohydrates 15g
protein 3g

Pumpernickel Bread In Bread Machine

Preparation Time: 10 minutes
Cooking Time: 3 hours 55 minutes
Servings: 14
Ingredients:
2 1/2 tsp of bread machine yeast
(Optional) 1 1/2 tbsp of vital wheat gluten
1 cup of whole wheat flour
1 cup of rye flour
1 1/2 cups of bread flour
(Optional) 1 tbsp of caraway seed
3 tbsp of cocoa
1/3 cup of molasses
1 1/2 tsp of salt
1 1/2 tbsp of vegetable oil
1 1/8 cups of warm water
Directions:
Combine all the bread ingredients in order suggested by manufacturer in the bread machine pan. Most bread machine recommend adding liquid first. Select Basic cycle or white bread function and press Start.

Once baked, Remove bread from pan, transfer onto wire rack and let cool before slicing.
Nutrition:
Calories: 119 kcal
Fat 2.3g
Carbohydrates 22.4g
protein 3.4g

Poppy Seed Roll

Preparation Time: 1 hour 30 minutes
Cooking Time: 1 hour 30 minutes
Servings: 1 roll / 8 slices
Ingredients:
For dough:
1 egg
1 cup (250 ml) water
2/3 cup (150 g, 5.3 oz) butter
½ cup (70 g, 2.5 oz) sugar
4 cups (500 g, 18 oz) all-purpose flour
1 tablespoon instant yeast
1 teaspoon salt
For the filling:
4 cups (500 g, 35.2 oz) poppy seeds
½ cup (125 ml, 4 oz) milk
¼ cup (50 g, 2 oz) butter
1 teaspoon cinnamon
¼ cup (50 g) hazelnuts, ground
1 egg
For garnish:
1 cup (200 g, 7.1 oz) sugar powder
2 tablespoons rum
Directions:
Knead the dough in a bread machine. Let it rest for 45 minutes.

Dip poppy seeds in boiling water for 5 minutes. Then add butter, cinnamon, hazelnuts, and egg. Mix the ingredients together. Let it cool.
Roll out the dough to make a rectangle (5 cm, 2 inches). Spread the poppy filling over the dough and roll it up.
Put the roll into the baking cup and place it in the bread maker. Leave for 30 minutes to rest and rise.
Turn on the BAKE mode and set the cooking time for 60 minutes.
Mix powdered sugar and rum for the icing.
Let the cooked roll slightly cool down, take it out of the cup, and immediately cover with the icing.
Slice, and serve.
Enjoy!
Nutrition:
Calories 943
Total Fat 54.1 g, Saturated Fat 16.8 g, Cholesterol 96 mg sodium474 mg, Total Carbohydrate 99 g, Dietary Fiber 9 g
Total Sugars 43.6 g
protein 21.4 g, Vitamin D 18 mcg, Calcium 957 mg, Iron 10 mg, Potassium 609 mg

Fruit Bread

Preparation Time: 1 hour 30 minutes
Cooking Time: 1 hour 30 minutes
Servings: 1 loaf / 8 slices
Ingredients:

1 egg
1 cup (250 ml) milk
2 tablespoons rum
¼ cup (60 g, 2 oz) butter
¼ cup (50 g, 1.9 oz) brown sugar
4 cups (500 g, 18 oz) all-purpose flour/bread flour
1 tablespoon instant yeast
1 teaspoon salt
Fruits:
¼ cups (50 g) dried apricots, coarsely chopped
¼ cups (50 g) prunes, coarsely chopped
¼ cups (50 g) candied cherry, pitted
½ cups (100 g) seedless raisins
¼ cup (50 g) almonds, chopped

Directions:
Add all of the ingredients to your bread machine (except fruits), carefully following the instructions of the manufacturer.
Set the program of your bread machine to BASIC/SWEET and set the crust type to LIGHT or MEDIUM.
Press START.
Once the machine beeps, add fruits.
Wait until the cycle completes.
Once the loaf is ready, take the bucket out and let the loaf cool for 5 minutes.
Gently shake the bucket to remove the loaf.
Transfer to a cooling rack, slice, and serve.
Enjoy!
Nutrition:
Calories 441

Total Fat 10.9 g, Saturated Fat 4.6 g, Cholesterol 38 mg sodium361 mg, Total Carbohydrate 74.9 g, Dietary Fiber 3.8 g
Total Sugars 20.3 g
protein 10.8 g, Vitamin D 6 mcg, Calcium 84 mg, Iron 4 mg, Potassium 332 mg

Marzipan Cherry Bread

Preparation Time: 1 hour 30 minutes
Cooking Time: 1 hour 30 minutes
Servings: 1 loaf / 8 slices
Ingredients:
1 egg
¾ cup (180 ml, 6 oz) milk
1 tablespoon almond liqueur
4 tablespoons orange juice
½ cup (100 g) ground almonds
¼ cup (60 g, 2 oz) butter
1/3 cup (80 g, 2.5 oz) sugar
4 cups (500 g, 18 oz) all-purpose flour/bread flour
1 tablespoon instant yeast
1 teaspoon salt
½ cup (150 g, 6 oz) marzipan
½ cup (100 g) dried cherries, pitted

Directions:
Add all of the ingredients to your bread machine (except marzipan and cherry), carefully following the instructions of the manufacturer.
Set the program of your bread machine to BASIC/SWEET and set the crust type to LIGHT or MEDIUM.
Press START.
Once the machine beeps, add marzipan and cherry.
Wait until the cycle completes.
Once the loaf is ready, take the bucket out and let the loaf cool for 5 minutes.
Gently shake the bucket to remove the loaf.
Transfer to a cooling rack, slice, and serve.
Enjoy!
Nutrition:
Calories 511
Total Fat 16.4 g, Saturated Fat 4.7 g, Cholesterol 38 mg sodium355 mg, Total Carbohydrate 77.3 g, Dietary Fiber 3.9 g
Total Sugars 10.8 g
protein 12.2 g, Vitamin D 6 mcg, Calcium 78 mg, Iron 4 mg, Potassium 240 mg

Coconut Milk Bread

Preparation Time: 1 hour 30 minutes
Cooking Time: 1 hour 30 minutes
Servings: 1 loaf / 8 slices

Ingredients:
1 egg
½ cup (100 ml, 4 oz) milk
½ cup (120 ml, 4 oz) coconut milk
¼ cup (50 g, 2 oz) butter
2 tablespoons (50 g) honey
4 cups (500 g, 18 oz) all-purpose flour/bread flour
1 tablespoon instant yeast
1 teaspoon salt
½ cup (100 g, 6 oz) coconut chips

Directions:
Add all of the ingredients to your bread machine (except coconut chips), carefully following the instructions of the manufacturer.
Set the program of your bread machine to BASIC/SWEET and set the crust type to LIGHT or MEDIUM.
Press START.
Once the machine beeps, add coconut chips.
Wait until the cycle completes.
Once the loaf is ready, take the bucket out and let the loaf cool for 5 minutes.
Gently shake the bucket to remove the loaf.
Transfer to a cooling rack, slice, and serve.
Enjoy!
Nutrition:
Calories 421
Total Fat 15.3 g, Saturated Fat 11.7 g, Cholesterol 37 mg sodium350 mg, Total Carbohydrate 61.9 g, Dietary Fiber 3.2 g
Total Sugars 11.7 g
protein 9.5 g, Vitamin D 6 mcg, Calcium 33 mg, Iron 4 mg, Potassium 157 mg

Liqueur Apple Pie

Preparation Time: 1 hour 30 minutes
Cooking Time: 1 hour 30 minutes
Servings: 10

Ingredients:
For dough:
1 egg
1 cup (250 ml, 8 oz) whole milk
¼ cup (60 g, 2 oz, ½ stick) butter
2 tablespoons (50 g) sugar
4 cups (500 g, 18 oz) all-purpose flour
1 tablespoon instant yeast
¼ teaspoon salt
For cream:
7/8 cup (200 ml, 7 oz) milk
2 tablespoons starch
2 tablespoons (50 g) sugar
2 eggs
½ cup (100 ml) egg liqueur
For filling:
2.2 pounds (1 kg) fresh apples
2 tablespoons lemon juice
For garnish:
1½ cups (100 g) almond, flaked
1/5 cup egg liqueur

Directions:

Knead the dough in a bread machine. Let it rest for 45 minutes.

To make the cream, combine milk, starch, and sugar. Keep stirring and bring it to a boil. Remove from heat and cool slightly.

Stir in some egg liqueur and 2 yolks.

Wash and peel the apples. Cut them into slices, and then sprinkle with lemon juice.

Take the dough out of the bread maker, roll it out evenly, and place it on a baking sheet covered with oiled parchment paper.

Evenly spread the cream over the dough and cover with apple slices in an overlapping manner.

Leave the pie in a warm place for 30 minutes to rest and rise.

Preheat the oven to 350 degrees F (180 degrees C).

Bake until golden brown (about 25-30 minutes).

For garnish, slightly roast almonds on a dry frying pan. Sprinkle them over the cake when it is still warm.

Sprinkle the pie with 1/5 cup (50 ml) of egg liqueur before serving.

Let the pie cool down, slice, and serve.

Enjoy!

Nutrition:

Calories 429

Total Fat 14.2 g, Saturated Fat 4.8 g, Cholesterol 67 mg

sodium132 mg, Total Carbohydrate 62.1 g, Dietary Fiber 3.4 g

Total Sugars 15.4 g

protein 11.6 g, Vitamin D 26 mcg, Calcium 96 mg, Iron 3 mg, Potassium 263 mg

Honey Nut Bread

Preparation Time: 1 hour 30 minutes

Cooking Time: 1 hour 30 minutes

Servings: 1 loaf / 8 slices

Ingredients:

2 eggs

2/3 cup (150 g, 5.3 oz) cottage cheese

½ cup (100 ml, 3.55 oz) milk

¼ cup (60 g, 2 oz) butter

2 tablespoons (60 g) honey

4 cups (500 g, 18 oz) all-purpose flour/bread flour

1 tablespoon instant yeast

1 teaspoon salt

¾ cup (100 g) candied nuts, chopped

Directions:

Add all of the ingredients to your bread machine (except nuts), carefully following the instructions of the manufacturer.

Set the program of your bread machine to BASIC/SWEET and set the crust type to LIGHT or MEDIUM.

Press START.

Once the machine beeps, add nuts.

Wait until the cycle completes. Once the loaf is ready, take the bucket out and let the loaf cool for 5 minutes.

Gently shake the bucket to remove the loaf.

Transfer to a cooling rack, slice, and serve.

Enjoy!

Nutrition:

Calories 422

Total Fat 13.9 g, Saturated Fat 5.2 g, Cholesterol 59 mg sodium450 mg, Total Carbohydrate 59.8 g, Dietary Fiber 2.8 g

Total Sugars 8.8 g protein 13.7 g, Vitamin D 8 mcg, Calcium 62 mg, Iron 4 mg, Potassium 143 mg

Spinach Salmon Pie

Preparation Time: 1 hour 30 minutes

Cooking Time: 1 hour 30 minutes

Servings: 10

Ingredients:

For dough:

1¼ cup (300 ml) water

3 tablespoons olive oil

3½ cups (500 g, 15¾ oz) whole grain flour

¼ teaspoon salt

1 package active dry yeast

For filling:

1.1 pounds (500 g) salmon fillet

2.2 pounds (1 kg) leaf spinach

1/3 cup (50 g) pine nuts

1 onion

2 garlic cloves

pepper

salt

For fill:

4 eggs

½ cup grated parmesan cheese

1 pinch salt

1 2/3 cups (400 ml) cream

1 lemon, zest, and juice

1 tablespoon mustard

pepper

For breading:

¼ cup (50 g) butter, softened

½ bunch of dills
1 cup (120 g, 4 oz) breadcrumbs

Directions:

Knead the dough in a bread machine. Let it rest for 45 minutes.

Roast pine nuts with chopped onion and garlic. Add chopped spinach leaves. When the mixture has reduced in volume, season it with salt and pepper. Cool the mixture down and strain the liquid.

Rinse the salmon fillet, let it drip dry, and cut into small pieces.

Take the dough out of the bread maker, roll it out evenly, and place it (forming a board) on a baking sheet covered with oiled parchment paper.

Spread the spinach filling over the dough surface, and put the salmon on top of that.

For the topping: stir eggs with dairy cream, and then season with salt, pepper, lemon zest, lemon juice, and mustard. Add grated cheese and pour over the cake.

Leave in a warm place for 20 minutes to rest and rise.

Preheat the oven to 400 degrees F (200 degrees C).

Bake the pie for 10 minutes.

For the coating: rinse the dill, let it dry, finely chop, and mix with butter and breadcrumbs. Evenly spread the coating over the cake surface.

Bake the pie for 20 minutes more.

Let the pie cool down.

Slice, serve, and enjoy!

Nutrition:

Calories 499

Total Fat 21.6 g, Saturated Fat 6.7 g, Cholesterol 108 mg sodium566 mg, Total Carbohydrate 54 g, Dietary Fiber 9.6 g

Total Sugars 2.7 g

protein 26.1 g, Vitamin D 9 mcg, Calcium 251 mg, Iron 5 mg, Potassium 610 mg

Tomato Quiche

Preparation Time: 1 hour 30 minutes
Cooking Time: 1 hour 30 minutes
Servings: 8

Ingredients:

For sponge:
4/5 cup (200 ml) milk
1/3 cup (80 ml) water
2 cups (250 g) whole grain flour
2 teaspoons (5 g) fresh yeast
For dough:
2 tablespoons (40 g) honey
cup (60 g, ½ stick) butter
2 cups (250 g, 8 oz) all-purpose flour
2 ½ tablespoon (25 g) fresh yeast
teaspoon salt
After beeping:
1 cup (100 g) sun-dried tomatoes, chopped
For filling:
0.9 pounds (400 g) fresh tomatoes
For fill:
1 cup (100 g, 3 oz) parmesan cheese
½ cup (50 g) Gouda cheese
1¼ cups (300 g) sour cream
2 eggs
pizza spicy mix
pepper
salt

Directions:

Put all ingredients for the bread-starter to the bread machine and start the program DOUGH. When the components have mixed well, stop the program. Let the dough rest and rise for 30 minutes.
Then add the dough ingredients. Set DOUGH mode again. Let the dough rest and rise for 45 minutes.
Wash tomatoes and cut them into thin slices.
Combine all the ingredients for the fill.
Take the dough out of the bread maker, roll it out evenly, and place it (forming a board) on a baking sheet covered with oiled parchment paper.
Cover with tomato slices and pour filling over the dough.
Let the pie rest and rise in a warm place for 30 minutes.
Preheat the oven to 400 degrees F (200 degrees C).
Bake until golden brown (about 25-30 minutes).
Let the cake cool down.
Slice, serve, and enjoy!

Nutrition:
Calories 485
Total Fat 22.3 g, Saturated Fat 13 g, Cholesterol 99 mg sodium415 mg, Total Carbohydrate 57.2 g, Dietary Fiber 9 g
Total Sugars 7.5 g
protein 19.9 g, Vitamin D 8 mcg, Calcium 274 mg, Iron 4 mg, Potassium 542 mg

Mexican Vegetable Tart

Preparation Time: 1 hour
Cooking Time: 1 hour
Servings: 10

Ingredients:

For dough:
1¼ cup (300 ml) water
3 tablespoons olive oil
3½ cups (500 g, 15¾ oz) whole grain flour
¼ teaspoon salt
1 package active dry yeast
1 teaspoon grounded chili pepper
For filling:
1 tablespoon mustard
2 cups corn grains, boiled
2 cups canned beans
½ pound (200 g) cherry tomatoes
2 tablespoons chili paste/sauce
1¾ cups (200 ml) sour cream
2 cups (200 g, 6 oz) parmesan cheese, grated

Directions:
Knead the dough in a bread machine. Let it rest for 45 minutes.
Wash tomatoes and dice them small. Add corn, beans, chili paste, and mustard. Stir the mixture.
Take the dough out of the bread maker, roll it out evenly, and place it (forming a board) on a baking sheet covered with oiled parchment paper.
Brush the dough surface with sour cream, evenly spread the filling, and then sprinkle with grated cheese.
Leave in a warm place for 30 minutes to rest and rise.
Preheat the oven to 400 degrees F (200 degrees C).
Bake the tart for 25-30 minutes (until golden brown).
Let the pie cool down.
Slice, serve, and enjoy!

Nutrition:
Calories 355
Total Fat 13.7 g, Saturated Fat 5.8 g, Cholesterol 22 mg sodium266 mg, Total Carbohydrate 47.3 g, Dietary Fiber 7.9 g
Total Sugars 2.8 g
protein 15.5 g, Vitamin D 0 mcg, Calcium 236 mg, Iron 3 mg, Potassium 352 mg

Pear Cheese Quiche

Preparation Time: 1 hour
Cooking Time: 1 hour
Servings: 8

Ingredients:

For dough:

1¼ cup (300 ml) water
3 tablespoons olive oil
3½ cups (500 g, 15¾ oz) whole grain flour
¼ teaspoon salt
1 package active dry yeast

For filling:

5 pears
5 tablespoons lemon juice
1¾ cup (400 g) Gorgonzola cheese
1 1/3 cup (300 g) cottage cheese
4 tablespoons apple cider vinegar
2 eggs
ground nutmeg
pepper
salt

Directions:

Knead the dough in a bread machine. Let it rest for 45 minutes.

Peel the pears and cut them into halves. Remove the cores, and then sprinkle the pears with lemon juice. Put them in a saucepan, cover with boiling water, cover with a lid, and cook for 5 minutes on low heat. Take the pears out and let them drain to dry.

In another bowl, mash gorgonzola with a fork, add full-fat cottage cheese, and then season with salt, pepper, and nutmeg. Stir in the eggs.

Take the dough out of the bread maker, roll it out evenly, and place it (forming a board) on a baking sheet covered with oiled parchment paper.

Cut the pear halves into thin slices and evenly lay them onto the dough surface. Spread the cheese mixture over the pears.

Leave in a warm place for 30 minutes to rest and rise.

Preheat the oven to 400 degrees F (200 degrees C).

Bake the tart for 25-30 minutes (until golden brown).

Slice, serve, and enjoy!

Nutrition:

Calories 559
Total Fat 22.6 g, Saturated Fat 11.2 g, Cholesterol 91 mg sodium873 mg, Total Carbohydrate 70.4 g, Dietary Fiber 13.5 g
Total Sugars 13.4 g
protein 26.9 g, Vitamin D 4 mcg, Calcium 300 mg, Iron 3 mg, Potassium 485 mg

Leek Quiche

Preparation Time: 1 hour
Cooking Time: 1 hour
Servings: 10

Ingredients:

For dough:

1¼ cup (300 ml) water

3 tablespoons oil

3½ cups (500 g, 15¾ oz) whole grain flour

¼ teaspoon salt

1 package active dry yeast

For filling:

1.65 pounds (750 g) leek

For fill:

1¼ cup (150 g) soft sheep cheese

1¾ cup (400 ml) cream

4 eggs

Nutmeg

Pepper

Salt

Directions:

Knead the dough in a bread machine. Let it rest for 45 minutes.

For the topping, wash the leeks, cut each leaf into halves lengthwise, and chop them into pieces (about 1 cm). Put the leeks into salted boiling water and cook for 2 minutes. Drain the leeks, rinse with cold water, and let them drain dry.

Grate the sheep cheese and then mix with whipped cream and eggs. Add onion, and then season with salt, pepper, and nutmeg.

Take the dough out of the bread maker, roll it out evenly, and place it (forming a board) on a baking sheet covered with oiled parchment paper.

Evenly spread the leek filling over the dough.

Leave in a warm place for 30 minutes to rest and rise.

Preheat the oven to 400 degrees F (200 degrees C).

Bake the tart for 25-30 minutes (until golden brown).

Let the pie cool down.

Slice, serve, and enjoy!

Nutrition:

Calories 324

Total Fat 10.2 g, Saturated Fat 3.4 g, Cholesterol 85 mg sodium219 mg, Total Carbohydrate 48.5 g, Dietary Fiber 7.6 g

Total Sugars 4.1 g

protein 13.6 g, Vitamin D 6 mcg, Calcium 154 mg, Iron 4 mg, Potassium 397 mg

Asparagus Ham Quiche

Preparation Time: 1 hour

Cooking Time: 1 hour

Servings: 8

Ingredients:

For dough:

1¼ cup (300 ml) water

3 tablespoons olive oil

3½ cups (500 g, 15¾ oz) whole grain flour

¼ teaspoon salt

1 package active dry yeast

For filling:

2½ pounds (1 kg) white asparagus

1 leek stem

1½ cup (360 ml) cream

12 asparagus pods

2 egg yolks

3 tablespoons capers

2 cups (200 g) parmesan cheese

Pepper

Salt

For garnish:

10 slices ham

Directions:

Knead the dough in a bread machine. Let it rest for 45 minutes.

Wash and peel the asparagus, cut it into 1½-inch (3-4 cm) pieces. Leave in boiling salted water for 5 minutes, and then drain the water.

Wash the leeks, cut the white parts into small dices, and slice the green stem.

Take the dough out of the bread maker, roll it out evenly, and place it (forming a board) on a baking sheet covered with oiled parchment paper.

Stir dairy cream and egg yolks, add the white leek pieces, and season with salt and pepper. Spread the mixture over the dough.

Evenly spread asparagus, leek, and capers over the top and cover with grated cheese.

Leave in a warm place for 30 minutes to rest and rise.

Preheat the oven to 400 degrees F (200 degrees C).

Bake the tart for 25-30 minutes (until golden brown).

Garnish the hot tart with ham slices and serve immediately. Enjoy!

Nutrition:

Calories 469

Total Fat 18.2 g, Saturated Fat 7.3 g, Cholesterol 97 mg sodium807 mg, Total Carbohydrate 56.3 g, Dietary Fiber 11.5 g

Total Sugars 4 g protein 27 g, Vitamin D 5 mcg, Calcium 309 mg, Iron 6 mg, Potassium 688 mg

Meat Quiche
Preparation Time: 1 hour
Cooking Time: 1 hour
Servings: 8
Ingredients:
For dough:
1¼ cup (300 ml) water
3 tablespoons oil
3½ cups (500 g, 15¾ oz) whole grain flour
¼ teaspoon salt
1 package active dry yeast
After beeping:
2 tablespoons sesame seeds
For filling:
1.1 pounds (500 g) ground meat
1 onion
2 bell peppers, finely chopped
6 tomatoes cherry
1 cup (250 ml) cream
1½ cup (150 g) parmesan, grated
2 tablespoons mustard
2 tablespoons ketchup
Species for pizza
Pepper
Salt

Directions:
Knead the dough in a bread machine. Let it rest for 45 minutes.
Season ground meat with salt, pepper, and herb flavors, and then fry with chopped onion.
Add dairy cream, mustard, and ketchup.
Take the dough out of the bread maker, roll it out evenly, and place it (forming a board) on a baking sheet covered with oiled parchment paper.

Evenly spread the ground meat over the dough. Put tomatoes and bell peppers on the top. Cover with grated cheese.
Leave in a warm place for 30 minutes to rest and rise.
Preheat the oven to 400 degrees F (200 degrees C).
Bake the tart for 25-30 minutes (until golden brown).
Let the pie cool down.
Slice, serve, and enjoy!
Nutrition:
Calories 509
Total Fat 21.3 g, Saturated Fat 7.8 g, Cholesterol 64 mg sodium275 mg, Total Carbohydrate 54.4 g, Dietary Fiber 9.4 g
Total Sugars 4.7 g
protein 30.1 g, Vitamin D 0 mcg, Calcium 252 mg, Iron 5 mg, Potassium 400 mg

Chicken Quiche

Preparation Time: 1 hour
Cooking Time: 1 hour
Servings: 8
Ingredients:
For dough:
1¼ cup (300 ml) water
3 tablespoons olive oil
3½ cups (500 g, 15¾ oz) whole grain flour
¼ teaspoon salt
1 package active dry yeast
For filling:
1.1 pounds (500 g) chicken breast
¼ cup (50 g) sugar
2 cups (240 g) cranberries
2 red onions, chopped
4 leek stalks, cut into circles
1¾ cup (400 ml) cream
1½ cup (150 g) parmesan, grated
3 tablespoons olive oil
Pepper
Directions:
Knead the dough in a bread machine. Let it rest for 45 minutes.
Boil the chicken until cooked (for about 20 minutes over low heat). Remove the bones, and cut the meat into slices.
Melt sugar in a frying pan, add washed cranberries, and stew for 3 minutes.
Take the dough out of the bread maker, roll it out evenly, and place it (forming a board) on a baking sheet covered with oiled parchment paper.
Cover the dough with the cream.

Evenly spread meat, cranberries, onion, and leek over the dough.
Sprinkle with grated cheese, oil, and pepper.
Leave in a warm place for 30 minutes to rest and rise.
Preheat the oven to 400 degrees F (200 degrees C).
Bake the tart for 25-30 minutes (until golden brown).
Let the pie cool down.
Slice, serve, and enjoy!
Nutrition:
Calories 540
Total Fat 19.7 g, Saturated Fat 5.8 g, Cholesterol 61 mg sodium233 mg, Total Carbohydrate 65.5 g, Dietary Fiber 10.3 g
Total Sugars 11.3 g
protein 29.5 g, Vitamin D 0 mcg, Calcium 240 mg, Iron 4 mg, Potassium 688 mg

American Sourdough Bread

Preparation Time: 20-30 minutes
Cooking Time: 30 minutes
Servings: Makes two loaves
Ingredients:
Two packets (1/4 ounce each) active dry yeast
1-1/4 cup hot water (110 ° to 115 °)
1 cup Sourdough Starter
Two eggs
1/4 cup sugar
1/4 cup vegetable oil
One teaspoon salt
Six to 6-1/2 cups of all-purpose flour
Melted butter

Directions:
Dissolve the yeast into warm water in a large tub. Add the starter Sourdough, milk, sugar, butter, salt, and 3 cup flour. Play to smooth. Stir the remaining flour in enough to form a soft dough.
Turn onto a floured surface knead for around 6-8 minutes, until smooth and elastic. Place them in a greased tub, rotating to grease the top once.
Conceal and let it rise until doubled in a warm spot for around 1 hour.
Punch-down the bread. Move onto a surface that is lightly floured
divide in half. Mold into loaves. Put in two 8x4-in greased tiles—Pans loaf. Cover and let it rise for about forty-five minutes until doubled.

Bake 30-35 minutes at 375 ° C, or until golden brown.
Remove the wire racks from the pans to cool—pinch sugar.
Nutrition:
1 slice: 113
Calories, 2 g of fat (0 saturated fat), 12 mg of cholesterol, 79 mg of sodium, 20 g of carbohydrate, and 3 g of protein.

Swedish Limpa Bread

Preparation Time: 30 minutes
Cooking Time: 30 minutes
Servings: Makes two loaves (12 slices each)

Ingredients:
1/2 cup of light brown sugar
1/4 cup of dark molasses
1/4 cup of butter
Two tablespoons of grated orange zest
1-1/2 teaspoons of salt
One teaspoon aniseed, lightly crushed
1 cup of boiling water
1 cup of cold water
Two packets (1/4 ounce each) of active dry yeast
Half cup or small mug of warm water (110 ° to 115 °)
4-1/2 cups of all-purpose flour
3 to 4 cups of rye flour
Two tablespoons of cornmeal
2 tbsp melted butter

Directions:
Add brown sugar, molasses, butter, orange zest, salt, aniseed, and boiling water in a large bowl

whisk until brown sugar is dissolved, and butter melted. Remove cold water
let stand until the mixture cools to 110 to 115 degrees. Meanwhile, mix the yeast in lukewarm water in a large tub. Mix in molasses
blend well. Add 1 cup rye flour and all-purpose flour. Beat for 3 minutes on medium speed. Remove enough remaining rye flour for a steep dough to shape.
Turn onto a floured surface knead for around 6-8 minutes, until smooth and elastic. Place them in a greased tub, turning to graze the top once. Conceal and let it rise until doubled in a warm spot, around 1 hour. Punch-down the bread. Put it on a place that is lightly floured
divide in half. In two oval loaves, shape. Grease two baking sheets, then sprinkle with cornmeal lightly—place loaves on prepared pans. Conceal and let rise, for about thirty minutes, till it doubles. The oven is to be preheated to 350 °. Make four shallow slashes through each loaf with a sharp knife—Bake for 30-35 minutes or until brown or golden. Remove to rack wire brush with butter.
Nutrition:
1 slice: 186
Calories, 3 g of fat (2 g of saturated fat), 8 mg of cholesterol, 172 mg of sodium, 35 g of carbohydrate (7 g of sugar, 3 g of fiber).

Chocolate chip loaf

Preparation Time: 30 minutes
Cooking Time: 35 minutes
Servings: Makes 1 loaf (16 slices)

Ingredients:

3 Big eggs, room temperature
1 cup of sugar
2 cups of sour cream
3 cups of self-rising flour
2 cups of chocolate chips, semi-sweet

Directions:

Preheat the oven until 350 °. Beat the eggs, sugar and sour cream until they blend well. Stir in flour, slowly. Fold them into chocolate chips. Move to a fatted 9x5-in. Loaf mold. Bake for sixty-five to seventy-five minutes until a toothpick comes out clean. Cool in a saucepan for 5 minutes before moving to a wire rack.
Note: Use 4-1/2 teaspoons of baking powder and 1-1/2 teaspoons of salt in a measuring cup as a replacement for 3 cups of self-rising flour. Combine with an additional 2 cups of all-purpose flour to weigh 1 cup.
Nutrition:
1 slice: 306 Calories, 13 g of fat (8 g of saturated fat), 42 mg of cholesterol, 305 mg of sodium, 44 g of carbohydrate (25 g of fiber), 5 g of protein.

Italian Ciambella

Preparation Time: 15 minutes
Cooking Time: 45 minutes
Servings: Makes one loaf (20 slices)

Ingredients:

4 cups of all-purpose flour
1 cup of sugar
Two tablespoons of rubbed orange zest
Three teaspoons of baking powder
Three large eggs, room temperature
1/2 cup 2% milk
1/2 cup olive oil
One large egg yolk,
One tablespoon of coarse sugar

Directions:

Preheat the oven until 350 °. Whisk the flour, sugar, orange peel and baking powder in a big cup.
Whisk eggs, milk, and oil in another pot until combined. Attach the mixture to the flour
just stir until moistened. Form a 6-in—the round loaf on a tray of greasy baking. Place egg yolk on top sprinkle with coarse sugar. Bake for forty-five to fifty minutes until a toothpick inserted in the center comes out clean. In the last 10 minutes, cover the top loosely with foil if necessary to avoid over-browning. Remove to wire rack from pan
serve warm.
Nutrition: 1 slice: 197 Calories, 7 g (1 g saturated fat), 38 mg cholesterol, 87 mg sodium, 30 g carbohydrate (11

g carbohydrates, 1 g fiber), and 4 g protein.

Italian Focaccia

Preparation Time: 30 minutes
Cooking Time: 15 minutes
Servings: Makes one loaf (8 wedges)

Ingredients:

1-1/8 teaspoons active dry yeast
Half cup of lukewarm water (110 ° to 115 °)
One tablespoon sugar
One tablespoon Italian seasoning
1/4 teaspoon salt
1/4 teaspoon pepper
1-1/3 to 1-2/3 cups of all-purpose flour
Two tablespoons of oil-packed sun-dried tomatoes, chopped
Two tablespoons of sweet red peppers, drained and chopped
Two tablespoons of ripe olives, drained
5 Greek olives, sliced
Five sliced green olives with peppers, drained
Two tablespoons of fresh parsley
One tablespoon of olive oil
One teaspoon of kosher salt
One teaspoon of Parmesan cheese
One teaspoon of roman cheese, shredded

Directions:

Dissolve the yeast into warm water in a large tub. Connect the sugar, Italian seasoning flavor, salt, pepper, and 1 cup flour. Beat to smooth. Stir the remaining flour in, enough to shape a healthy dough. Then place in the onions, chili peppers, olives, and parsley. Turn onto a floured surface knead for around 6-8 minutes, until smooth and elastic. Place them in a greased tub, turning to graze the top once. Conceal and let it rise until doubled in a warm spot, about 50 minutes.

Punch-down the bread. Form in a 9-in. Circle on the baking sheet, greased. Conceal and let rise in a warm area for about 25 minutes, until doubled. Make many dimples over top of the dough with your fingertips. Wash with olive oil. Sprinkle the cheeses and kosher salt.

Bake for about 14-18 minutes at 400 ° C, or until golden brown. Drop onto a rack of wire.

Your scrumptious Italian Focaccia is ready!

Nutrition: One wedge: 118 Calories, 3 g fat (0 saturated fat), 0 cholesterol, 418 mg sodium, 19 g carbohydrate, 3 g protein.

The United Kingdom Hot-Crossed Buns

Preparation Time: 25 minutes
Cooking Time: 15 minutes
Servings: Makes 2-1/2 dozen

Ingredients:

Two packets (1/4 ounce each) active dry yeast
2 cups warm whole milk (110 ° to 115 °)
Two large eggs
1/3 cup butter softened
1/4 cup sugar
1-1/2 teaspoon salt
One teaspoon ground cinnamon
1/4 teaspoon ground allspice
6 to 7 cups all-purpose flour
1/2 cup dried currants
1/2 cup raisins
One large egg yolk
Two tablespoons water
Icing:
1-1/2 cup sugar
4 to 6 teaspoons of whole milk

Directions:

Dissolve yeast into the warm milk in a small cup. Combine the eggs, butter, sugar, salt, spices, yeast mixture and 3 cups of flour in a wide bowl beat until smooth at a medium pace. Add currants, raisins, and ample remaining flour to form a soft dough (the dough will be sticky). Put onto a floured part knead for about 6-8 minutes, until dough is smooth and elastic. Place them in a greased tub, rotating to graze the top once. Conceal with plastic wrap and let it rise until doubled in a warm spot, around 1 hour.

Punch the dough in. Turn onto a floured surface break and form into 30 balls— place in 2. Detach from greased baking sheets. Cover with towels in the kitchen allow to rise in a warm place until doubled, 30-45 min. Preheat the oven until 375 ° C.

Cut a cross on above of each bun, using a sharp knife. Beat egg yolk and water in a small utensil
brush over tops—Bake for 15-20 minutes or until golden

brown. Lift the racks from pans to wire to cool slightly. For the icing, blend sugar from confectioners and enough milk in a small bowl to achieve desired consistency. Pipe a cross over the prepared bread-buns. Serve hot.

Nutrition:

1 bun: 171

Calories, 3 g fat, 28 mg cholesterol, 145 mg sodium, 31 g carbohydrate, 1 g sugar, 4 g protein.

Eastern Europe Rye Bread

Preparation Time: 25 minutes
Cooking Time: 35 minutes
Servings: Makes two loaves (12 slices each)

Ingredients:

2 Packets (1/4 ounce each) active dry yeast
1-1/2 cup warm water (110 ° to 115 °)
1/2 cup molasses
Six tablespoons butter softened
2 cup rye flour
1/4 cup baking cocoa
Two tablespoons caraway seeds
Two teaspoons salt
3-1/2 to 4 cups all-purpose flour
Cornmeal

Directions:

Dissolve the yeast into warm water in a deep tub. Shake all-purpose flour in the molasses, sugar, rye meal, cocoa, caraway seeds, salt, and 2 cups until smooth. Incorporate enough remaining all-purpose flour to form a solid dough.

Turn onto a floured surface knead for 6-8 minutes, until smooth and elastic. Place them in a greased tub, rotating to grease top once. Cover and let stand until doubled in a warm spot, around 1-1/2 hours. Punch-down the prepared dough. Move onto a side that is lightly floured divide in half. Form each piece into about 10 in. Loaf. Big! Big! Grease 2 baking sheets and sprinkle some breadcrumbs—place loaves on prepared pans. Cover and let rise for around 1 hour, until doubled.

Bake at three-fifty ° for thirty to forty-five minutes, or when pressed, until the bread sounds hollow. Remove the wire racks from the pans to cool.

Nutrition:

1 slice: 146

Calories, 3 g of fat (2 g of saturated fat), 8 mg of cholesterol, 229 mg of sodium,

26 g of carbohydrate (5 g of fiber), 3 g of protein.

Irish Soda Bread
Preparation Time: 15 minutes
Cooking Time: 30 minutes
Servings: Makes eight slices
Ingredients:
2 cups of all-purpose flour
Two tablespoons of brown sugar
One teaspoon baking powder
One teaspoon baking soda
1/2 teaspoon salt
Three tablespoons of cold butter
Two big eggs, room temperature, separated
1/3 cup raisins
3/4 cup buttermilk
Directions:
Preheat the oven until 375 °.
Whisk the first five ingredients together. Cut in butter until coarse crumbs match the mixture. Whisk one egg and buttermilk together in another tub. Attach the combination to the flour
just stir until moistened. Pour in the raisins.
Turn the floured surface gently knead six to eight times. Shape to a 6-1/2-in. Square loaf. Place it on a baking sheet that has been greased. Create a shallow cross on top of the loaf using a sharp knife.
Whisk remaining egg
brush over the top.
Bake, for 30-35 minutes, until golden brown. Move from pan to rack. Serve dry.

Nutrition:
1 piece: 210
Calories, 6 g of fat (3 g of saturated fat), 59 mg of cholesterol, 463 mg of sodium, 33 g of carbohydrate (8 g of sugar, 1 g of fiber).

Slovenia Poteca

Preparation Time: 25 minutes
Cooking Time: 1 hour
Servings: Makes 12 servings

Ingredients:

1 cup butter
1/2 cup 2 percent milk
Three large egg yolks, room temperature
Two packages (1/4 ounce each) active dry yeast
One-fourth cup warm water (110 ° to 115 °)
2-1/2 cups of all-purpose flour
1 1/4 teaspoon sugar
Salt

Filling:

2 cups ground walnuts
2 cups cut dates
1/4 cup 2 percent milk
Three tablespoons plus 1 cup sugar
1/2 teaspoon ground cinnamon
Three big white eggs, room temperature
Confectioner's sugar, optional

Directions:

Melt the butter with the milk in a small saucepan. Add egg yolks when mixed. Dissolve yeast in warm water in a small saucepan.

Mix the flour, sugar, and salt in a huge bowl
add butter and yeast mixture. Beat for 3 minutes on medium speed (the dough will be sticky): cover, and cold overnight.

Combine the nuts, dates, milk, three tablespoons of sugar, and cinnamon in a small saucepan over medium heat. Cook and stir until a paste forms a mixture. Shift to a big bowl.

In a small saucepan, beat egg whites until soft peaks form. Gradually, beat one tablespoon at a time in remaining sugar, on high peaks until stiff peaks develop. Fold into nut mixture.

Cut dough in half
on a floured surface, roll one portion into a 20-inch square. Spread half the filling over. Roll up tightly jelly- style. Place, seam side up, into a 10-in greased pan. Place, seam side down, over the first roll-up in the pan (layers will bake as one loaf).

Bake at 350 ° for 60-70 minutes, until golden brown. Leave for 10 minutes to cool completely before removing from pan onto the wire rack. Sprinkle some confectioner's sugar, if necessary.

Nutrition:

1 slice: 509
Calories, 26 g fat (11 g saturated fat), 92 mg cholesterol, 182 mg sodium, 66 g carbohydrate (41 g carbohydrates, 4 g fiber), and 8 g protein.

Chapter 14 Desserts

Apple Butter Bread
Preparation Time: 10 minutes
Cooking Time: 20-30 minutes
Servings: Makes 1 loaf
Ingredients:
8 SLICES / 1 POUND
⅔ cup milk, at 80°F to 90°F
⅓ cup apple butter, at room temperature
4 teaspoons melted butter, cooled
2 teaspoons honey
⅔ teaspoon salt
⅔ cup whole-wheat flour
1½ cups white bread flour
1 teaspoon bread machine or instant yeast
12 SLICES / 1½ POUNDS
1 cup milk, at 80°F to 90°F
½ cup apple butter, at room temperature
2 tablespoons melted butter, cooled
1 tablespoon honey
1 teaspoon salt
1 cup whole-wheat flour
2¼ cups white bread flour
1½ teaspoons bread machine or instant yeast
16 SLICES / 2 POUNDS
1⅓ cups milk, at 80°F to 90°F
⅔ cup apple butter, at room temperature
2⅔ tablespoons melted butter, cooled
4 teaspoons honey
1⅓ teaspoons salt
1⅓ cups whole-wheat flour
3 cups white bread flour

2 teaspoons bread machine or instant yeast
Directions:
Place the ingredients in your bread machine as recommended by the manufacturer.
Program the machine for Basic/White bread, select light or medium crust, and press Start.
When the loaf is done, remove the bucket from the machine. Let the loaf cool for 5 minutes.
Gently shake the bucket to remove the loaf, and turn it out onto a rack to cool.
Nutrition:
Calories: 178
Total Fat : 3g
Saturated Fat: 2g
Carbohydrates: 34g
fiber: 1g
Sodium: 220mg
Protein: 4g

Sweet Molasses Wheat Bread
Preparation Time: 30-45 minutes
Cooking Time: 30-45 minutes
Servings: Makes 1 loaf
Ingredients:
½ cup water at 80 degrees F
¼ cup milk at 80 degrees F
2 teaspoons melted butter, cooled
2 tablespoons honey
1 tablespoon molasses
1 teaspoon sugar
1 tablespoon skim milk powder

½ teaspoon salt
1 teaspoon unsweetened cocoa powder
1¼ cups whole wheat flour
1 cup white bread flour
1 teaspoon instant yeast

Directions:
Add all of the ingredients to your bread machine, carefully following the instructions of the manufacturer.
Set the program of your bread machine to Basic/White Bread and set crust type to Medium.
Press START.
Wait until the cycle completes.
Once the loaf is ready, take the bucket out and let the loaf cool for 5 minutes.
Gently shake the bucket to remove the loaf.
Transfer to a cooling rack, slice, and serve.
Nutrition: Total Carbs: 34g,
Fiber: 2g
protein: 4
fat: 2g,
Calories: 164

Lemon Peanut Bread
Preparation Time: 30 minutes
Cooking Time: 4 hours
Servings: 2 pounds / 20 slices
Ingredients:
1 cup lukewarm milk (80 degrees F)
3 cups wheat bread flour
½ cup peanut butter
1½ teaspoon active dry yeast
1 tablespoon powdered milk
1 lemon zest
1 whole egg
1 tablespoon walnut oil

Directions:
Prepare all of the ingredients for your bread and measuring means (a cup, a spoon, kitchen scales).
Carefully measure the ingredients into the pan, except the zest.
Place all of the ingredients, into the bread bucket in the right order, following the manual for your bread machine.
Close the cover.
Select the program of your bread machine to FRENCH and choose the crust color to LIGHT.
Press START.
After the signal, add the zest to the dough.
Wait until the program completes.
When done, take the bucket out and let it cool for 5-10 minutes.
Shake the loaf from the pan and let cool for 30 minutes on a cooling rack.
Slice, serve and enjoy the taste of fragrant homemade bread.
Nutrition:
Calories 314
Total Fat 11.5g
Saturated Fat 2.6g
Cholesterol 23mg
Sodium 103mg
Total Carbohydrate 42.5g
Dietary Fiber 2.6g
Total Sugars 4.5g
Protein 11.3g

Cauliflower Breadsticks

Preparation Time: 10 minutes
Cooking Time: 35 minutes
Servings: 8

Ingredients:

2 cups riced cauliflower
1 cup mozzarella, shredded
1 tsp. Italian seasoning
2 eggs
½ tsp. ground pepper
1 tsp. salt
½ tsp. granulated garlic
¼ cup Parmesan cheese as a topping

Directions:

Preheat the oven to 350F.
Grease a baking sheet.
Beat the eggs until mixed well.
Combine rice, cauliflower, mozzarella cheese, Italian seasoning, pepper, garlic, and salt and blend on low speed in a food processor. Combine with eggs.
Pour the dough into the prepared cookie sheet and pat the dough down to ¼ thick across the pan.
Bake for 30 minutes and dust the breadsticks with the parmesan cheese.
Put the breadsticks on the broil setting for 2 to 3 minutes, so the cheese melts.
Slice and serve.
Nutrition:
Calories: 165
fat: 10g, Carb: 5g
protein: 13g

Lemony Parmesan Breadsticks

Preparation Time: 20 minutes
Cooking Time: 25 minutes
Servings: 16

Ingredients:

1 tablespoon sugar
1 (1/4-ounce) package active dry yeast
1 cup warm water
1 cup bran cereal
2 1/4 cups all-purpose flour
1/2 cup Parmesan cheese, shredded
1 1/2 teaspoons lemon peel, grated
1 teaspoon garlic salt
1 teaspoon black pepper
1/2 teaspoon cayenne pepper
2 tablespoons olive oil
Cornmeal, as required
1 egg white, slightly beaten

Directions:

In a bowl, add sugar, yeast and warm water and mix until well blended. Set aside for about 5 minutes.

In a food processor, add cereal and pulse until crushed. Add flour, cheese, lemon peel, garlic salt, black pepper and cayenne pepper and pulse for about 10 seconds. Add oil and pulse for about 10 seconds more. Add yeast mixture and pulse a dough ball is formed. Set aside in processor for about 5 minutes. Again, pulse for about 10 seconds more. Remove the dough from the processor and place into a bowl. With a plastic wrap, cover the bowl and set aside for about 10 minutes.

Preheat the oven to 325 degrees F. Grease 2 baking sheets.

Cut the dough into 16 equal sized pieces. Place the dough pieces onto a cornmeal dusted surface and roll each into a thin and 14-inch long rope. Arrange the breadsticks onto prepared baking sheets in a single layer. Coat the top of each breadstick with egg white and set aside for about 15 minutes.

Bake for about 25-35 minutes or until top becomes golden brown.

Remove from the oven and place the baking sheets onto wire racks to cool completely before serving.

Nutrition:
Calories: 122
Total Fat: 3.5g
Saturated Fat: 1.2g
Protein: 4.6g
Carbs: 19.1g
fiber: 2g
Sugar: 1.6g

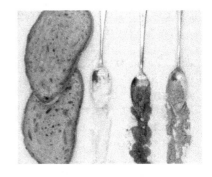

Molasses Breadsticks

Preparation Time: 20 minutes
Cooking Time: 18 minutes
Servings: 12

Ingredients:
2 tablespoons brown sugar
1 cup warm water
1 (¼-ounce) package dry yeast
1½-2 cups bread flour
1½ cups whole-wheat
flour
½ cup plus 2 tablespoons
cornmeal
2 tablespoons light
molasses
2 tablespoons butter, melted
2 eggs
1½ teaspoons salt
1 tablespoon cold water

Directions:
For breadsticks: in the bowl of
a stand mixer, dissolve brown
sugar and yeast in warm water.
Add ½ cup of bread flour,
wheat flour, ½ cup of
cornmeal, molasses, butter, 1
egg and salt and beat on
medium speed until smooth.
Add enough remaining bread
flour and beat until a dough
forms.
Place the dough onto a floured
surface and with your hands,
knead until smooth and
elastic. Now, transfer the
dough into a well-greased bowl
and turn to coat. With a
plastic wrap, cover the bowl
and set aside in a warm place
for about 1 hour.
With your hands, punch the
dough down. Arrange the
dough onto a floured surface
and cut into 12 pieces. Shape
each dough piece into 9x½-
inch breadsticks. Arrange the
breadsticks onto greased
baking sheets about 2-inch
apart. With a plastic wrap,
cover each baking sheet and
set aside in warm place for
about 20-30 minutes.
Preheat the oven to 375
degrees F.
Meanwhile, for egg wash: in a
bowl, add egg and 1
tablespoon of cold water and
beat well. Coat the breadsticks
with egg mixture and sprinkle
with cornmeal.
Bake for about 13-18 minutes
or until top becomes golden
brown.
Remove from the oven and
place the baking sheets onto
wire racks to cool completely.
Nutrition:
Calories: 177
Total Fat: 3.2g
Saturated Fat: 1.5g
Protein: 4.8g
Carbs: 31g
fiber: 1.3g
Sugar: 3.5g

Mustard Rye Bread

Preparation Time: 10 minutes
Cooking Time: 20-30 minutes
Servings: Makes 1 loaf

Ingredients:
8 SLICES / 1 POUND
¾ cup plus 1 tablespoon water,
at 80°F to 90°F

2⅔ tablespoons Dijon mustard
1 tablespoon melted butter,
cooled

2 teaspoons sugar
½ teaspoon salt
1 cup rye flour
1⅓ cups white bread flour
¾ teaspoon bread machine or instant yeast
12 SLICES / 1½ POUNDS
1¼ cups water, at 80°F to 90°F
¼ cup Dijon mustard
1½ tablespoons melted butter, cooled
1 tablespoon sugar
¾ teaspoon salt
1½ cups rye flour
2 cups white bread flour
1 teaspoon bread machine or instant yeast
16 SLICES / 2 POUNDS
1⅔ cups water, at 80°F to 90°F
¼ cup plus 4 teaspoons Dijon mustard
2 tablespoons melted butter, cooled
4 teaspoons sugar
1 teaspoon salt
2 cups rye flour
2⅔ cups white bread flour
1½ teaspoons bread machine or instant yeast

Directions:
Place the ingredients in your bread machine as recommended by the manufacturer.
Program the machine for Basic/White bread, select light or medium crust, and press Start.
When the loaf is done, remove the bucket from the machine.
Let the loaf cool for 5 minutes.

Gently shake the bucket to remove the loaf, and turn it out onto a rack to cool.
Nutrition:
Calories: 149
Total Fat : 2g
Saturated Fat: 1g
Carbohydrates: 28g
fiber: 4g
Sodium: 217mg
Protein: 5g

Once the loaf is ready, take the bucket out and let the loaf cool for 5 minutes.
Gently shake the bucket to remove the loaf.
Transfer to a cooling rack, slice, and serve.
Nutrition: Total Carbs: 29g,
Fiber: 1g
protein: 4g
fat: 2g,
Calories: 144

Simple Dark Rye Loaf

Preparation Time: 30-45 minutes
Cooking Time: 30-45 minutes
Servings: Makes 1 loaf
Ingredients:
⅔ Cup water at 80 degrees F
1 tablespoon melted butter, cooled
¼ cup molasses
¼ teaspoon salt
1 tablespoon unsweetened cocoa powder
½ cup rye flour
Pinch of ground nutmeg
1¼ cups white bread flour
1½ teaspoons instant yeast
Directions:
Add all of the ingredients to your bread machine, carefully following the instructions of the manufacturer.
Set the program of your bread machine to Basic/White Bread and set crust type to Medium.
Press START.
Wait until the cycle completes.

Honey Rye Bread

Preparation Time: 30-45 minutes
Cooking Time: 30-45 minutes
Servings: Makes 1 loaf
Ingredients:
2 ¼ cups (350 g) wheat flour
¼ cup (50 g) rye flour
1 cup (200 ml) lukewarm water
1 egg
1 tablespoon olive oil
1 teaspoon salt
1 ½ tablespoon liquid honey
1 teaspoon active dry yeast
Directions:
Prepare all of the ingredients for your bread and measuring means (a cup, a spoon, kitchen scales).
Carefully measure the ingredients into the pan.
Place all of the ingredients into the bread bucket in the right order, following the manual for your bread machine.
Close the cover.
Select the program of your bread machine to BASIC and

choose the crust color to
MEDIUM or DARK.
Press START.
Wait until the program
completes.
When done, take the bucket
out and let it cool for 5-10
minutes.
Shake the loaf from the pan
and let cool for 30 minutes on
a cooling rack.
Slice, serve and enjoy the taste
of fragrant homemade bread.
Nutrition:
Calories 177
Total Fat 2.7g
Saturated Fat 0.6g
Cholesterol 20g
Sodium 300mg
Total Carbohydrate 33.1g
Dietary Fiber 2.0g
Total Sugars 3.4g
Protein 5.1g

Raisin Bread

Preparation Time: 30 minutes
Cooking Time: 3 hours 10
minutes
Servings: Makes 1 loaf
Ingredients:
1/3 cup lukewarm milk (80
degrees F)
2 whole eggs
4 teaspoons butter, melted and
cooled
3 tablespoons sugar
2/3 teaspoons salt
1½ teaspoon lemon zest
2 cups all-purpose flour, sifted
1 1/3 teaspoons active dry
yeast
¼ cup slivered almonds
¼ cup seedless raisins

Directions:
Prepare all of the ingredients
for your bread and measuring
means (a cup, a spoon, kitchen
scales).
Carefully measure the
ingredients into the pan,
except the raisins and nuts.
Place all of the ingredients,
into the bread bucket in the
right order, following the
manual for your bread
machine.
Close the cover.
Select the program of your
bread machine to BASIC and
choose the crust color to
MEDIUM.
Press START.
After the signal, add the
raisins and nuts to the dough.
Wait until the program
completes.
When done, take the bucket
out and let it cool for 5-10
minutes.
Shake the loaf from the pan
and let cool for 30 minutes on
a cooling rack.
Slice, serve and enjoy the taste
of fragrant homemade bread.
Nutrition:
Calories 204
Total Fat 5.2g
Saturated Fat 1.9g
Cholesterol 47g
Sodium 228mg
Total Carbohydrate 33.7g
Dietary Fiber 1.6g
Total Sugars 8.1g
Protein 6.2g, Vitamin D 9mcg,
Calcium 34mg, Iron 2mg,
Potassium 122mg

Great British Muffin Bread

Preparation Time: 30-45 minutes
Cooking Time: 30-45 minutes
Servings: Makes 1 loaf
Ingredients:
⅔ cup buttermilk at 80 degrees F
1 tablespoon melted butter, cooled
1 tablespoon sugar
¾ teaspoon salt
¼ teaspoon baking powder
1¾ cups white bread flour
1½ teaspoons instant yeast
Directions:
Add all of the ingredients to your bread machine, carefully following the instructions of the manufacturer.
Set the program of your bread machine to Basic/White Bread and set crust type to Medium. Press START.
Wait until the cycle completes. Once the loaf is ready, take the bucket out and let the loaf cool for 5 minutes.
Gently shake the bucket to remove the loaf.
Transfer to a cooling rack, slice, and serve.
Nutrition: Total Carbs: 24g,
Fiber: 2g
protein: 4g
fat: 2g,
Calories: 131

Cream Cheese Muffins

Preparation Time: 15 minutes
Cooking Time: 15 minutes
Servings: 6
Ingredients:
1 cup all-purpose flour
½ cup cream cheese, softened
½ cup unsalted butter, softened
1 teaspoon baking powder
½ teaspoon salt
½ teaspoon smoked paprika
¾ cup milk
Directions:
Preheat the oven to 425 degrees F and line 6 cups of a muffin pan with silicone liners.
In the bowl of an electric mixer, place all the ingredients except milk and beat on medium-high speed for about 2 minutes. Slowly, add milk, beating continuously until well blended.
Transfer the cheese mixture into the prepared muffin cups evenly.
Bake for about 12-15 minutes or until top becomes golden brown.
Remove from the oven and place the pan onto a wire rack to cool for about 10 minutes. Carefully invert the muffins and place onto the wire rack to cool completely before serving.
Nutrition:
Calories: 296
Total Fat: 22.9g
Saturated Fat: 14.4g
Protein: 4.8g
Carbs: 18.4g
fiber: 0.7g

Sugar: 1.5g

Chocolate Muffins

Preparation Time: 15 minutes
Cooking Time: 20 minutes
Servings: 12

Ingredients:

2 cups all-purpose flour
1 cup white sugar
½ cup unsweetened cocoa powder
1 teaspoon baking soda
1 cup plain yogurt
½ cup milk
½ cup vegetable oil
1 egg
1 teaspoon vanilla extract
1 cup chocolate chips

Directions:

Preheat oven to 400 degrees F and grease 12 cups of a muffin pan.

In a large bowl, place the flour, sugar, cocoa powder and baking soda and mix well. In another bowl, add yogurt, milk, oil, egg and vanilla and beat until smooth. Add egg mixture into the bowl of flour mixture and mix until just blended. Gently, fold in ¾ cup f chocolate chips.

Place mixture into prepared muffin cups about ¾ of full and sprinkle with remaining chocolate chips.

Bake for 20 minutes or until a skewer inserted in the center of the muffins comes out clean.

Remove from the oven and place the pan onto a wire rack to cool for about 10 minutes.

Carefully invert the muffins and place onto the wire rack to cool completely before serving.

Nutrition:
Calories: 328
Total Fat: 14.7g
Saturated Fat: 5.5g
Protein: 5.9g
Carbs: 44.8g
fiber: 2.9g
Sugar: 26g

Delicious Italian Bread

Preparation Time: 30-45 minutes
Cooking Time: 30-45 minutes
Servings: Makes 1 loaf

Ingredients:

⅔ cup water at 80 degrees F
1 tablespoon olive oil
1 tablespoon sugar
¾ teaspoon salt
2 cups white bread flour
1 teaspoon instant yeast

Directions:

Add all of the ingredients to your bread machine, carefully following the instructions of the manufacturer.

Set the program of your bread machine to Basic/White Bread and set crust type to Medium. Press START.
Wait until the cycle completes. Once the loaf is ready, take the bucket out and let the loaf cool for 5 minutes.
Gently shake the bucket to remove the loaf.
Transfer to a cooling rack, slice, and serve.
Nutrition: Total Carbs: 26g,
Fiber: 1g
protein: 3g
fat: 2g,
Calories: 136

Original Italian Herb Bread

Preparation Time: 30-45 minutes
Cooking Time: 30-45 minutes
Servings: Makes 1 loaf
Ingredients:
1 cup water at 80 degrees F
½ cup olive brine
1½ tablespoons butter
3 tablespoons sugar
2 teaspoons salt
5⅓ cups flour
2 teaspoons bread machine yeast
20 olives, black/green
1½ teaspoons Italian herbs
Directions:
Cut olives into slices.
Add all of the ingredients to your bread machine (except olives), carefully following the instructions of the manufacturer.

Set the program of your bread machine to French Bread and set crust type to Medium. Press START.
Once the maker beeps, add olives.
Wait until the cycle completes. Once the loaf is ready, take the bucket out and let the loaf cool for 5 minutes.
Gently shake the bucket to remove the loaf.
Transfer to a cooling rack, slice, and serve.
Nutrition: Total Carbs: 71g,
Fiber: 1g
protein: 10g
fat: 7g,
Calories: 386

Italian Onion Bread

Preparation Time: 30-45 minutes
Cooking Time: 30-45 minutes
Servings: Makes 1 loaf
Ingredients:
1 cup warm milk, at room temperature
1 large whole egg
2 tablespoons butter, soft
¼ cup dried onion, minced
1½ teaspoons salt
2 tablespoons dried parsley flakes
1 teaspoon dried oregano
3½ cups bread flour
2 teaspoons dry yeast
Directions:
Add all of the ingredients to your bread machine, carefully following the instructions of the manufacturer

Set the program of your bread machine to Basic/White Bread and set crust type to Light
Press START
Wait until the cycle completes
Once the loaf is ready, take the bucket out and let the loaf cool for 5 minutes
Gently shake the bucket to remove the loaf
Transfer to a cooling rack, slice and serve
Enjoy!
Nutrition: Total Carbs: 23g,
Fiber: 1g
protein: 5g
fat: 2g,
Calories: 125

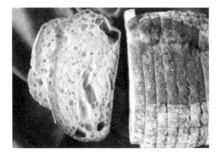

Orange Almond Loaf
Preparation Time: 30-45 minutes
Cooking Time: 30-45 minutes
Servings: Makes 1 loaf
Ingredients:
4 cups flour
¾ cup sweet almonds, chopped
3 tablespoons brown sugar
Peels of 2 oranges, grated
1 cup orange juice
2 tablespoons sweet almond oil
1 teaspoon salt

Powdered sugar for sprinkling
2½ bread machine yeast
Directions:
Add all of the ingredients to your bread machine (except the powdered sugar and ¼ cup of almonds), carefully following the instructions of the manufacturer.
Set the program of your bread machine to Basic/White Bread and set crust type to Medium.
Press START.
Wait until the cycle completes.
Once the loaf is ready, take the bucket out and let the loaf cool for 5 minutes.
Gently shake the bucket to remove the loaf.
Moisten the surface with water and sprinkle with remaining almonds and powdered sugar.
Transfer to a cooling rack, slice, and serve.
Nutrition: Total Carbs: 61.1g,
Fiber: 1g
protein: 8.5g
fat: 7g,
Calories: 347

Ricotta & Chive Loaf

Preparation Time: 30-45 minutes
Cooking Time: 30-45 minutes
Servings: Makes 1 loaf

Ingredients:
1 cup lukewarm water
1/3 cup whole ricotta cheese
1½ teaspoons salt
1 tablespoon granulated sugar
3 cups bread flour
½ cup chopped chives
2½ teaspoons instant yeast

Directions:
Add all of the ingredients to your bread machine, carefully following the instructions of the manufacturer (except dried fruits).
Set the program of your bread machine to Basic/White Bread and set crust type to Light.
Press START.
Once the machine beeps, add fruits.
Wait until the cycle completes.
Once the loaf is ready, take the bucket out and let the loaf cool for 5 minutes.
Gently shake the bucket to remove the loaf.
Transfer to a cooling rack, slice, and serve.
Enjoy!
Nutrition: Total Carbs: 17g,
Fiber: 1g
protein: 3g
fat: 0g,
Calories: 92

White Chocolate Cranberry Bread

Preparation Time: 10 minutes
Cooking Time: 20-30 minutes
Servings: Makes 1 loaf

Ingredients:
8 SLICES / 1 POUND
½ cup plus 1 tablespoon milk, at 80°F to 90°F
1 egg, at room temperature
1 tablespoon melted butter, cooled
⅔ teaspoon pure vanilla extract
4 teaspoons sugar
½ teaspoon salt
2 cups white bread flour
¾ teaspoon bread machine or instant yeast
⅓ cup white chocolate chips
¼ cup sweetened dried cranberries
12 SLICES / 1½ POUNDS
¾ cup plus 2 tablespoons milk, at 80°F to 90°F

1 egg, at room temperature
1½ tablespoons melted butter, cooled
1 teaspoon pure vanilla extract
2 tablespoons sugar
¾ teaspoon salt
3 cups white bread flour
1 teaspoon bread machine or instant yeast
½ cup white chocolate chips
⅓ cup sweetened dried cranberries
16 SLICES / 2 POUNDS
1 cup plus 3 tablespoons milk, at 80°F to 90°F
1 egg, at room temperature
2 tablespoons melted butter, cooled
1½ teaspoons pure vanilla extract
2⅔ tablespoons sugar
1 teaspoon salt
4 cups white bread flour
1⅓ teaspoons bread machine or instant yeast
⅔ cup white chocolate chips
½ cup sweetened dried cranberries

Directions:
Place the ingredients, except the chocolate chips and cranberries, in your bread machine as recommended by the manufacturer.
Program the machine for Basic/White bread, select light or medium crust, and press Start.
Add the white chocolate chips and cranberries when the machine signals or 5 minutes before the last knead cycle ends.

When the loaf is done, remove the bucket from the machine. Let the loaf cool for 5 minutes.
Gently shake the bucket to remove the loaf, and turn it out onto a rack to cool.
Nutrition:
Calories: 201
Total Fat : 5g
Saturated Fat: 3g
Carbohydrates: 34g
fiber: 1g
Sodium: 179mg
Protein: 5g

Chocolate Chip Peanut Butter Banana Bread

Preparation Time: 20 minutes
Cooking Time: 30-45 minutes
Servings: Makes 1 loaf
Ingredients:
12 TO 16 SLICES / 1½ TO 2 POUNDS
2 bananas, mashed
2 eggs, at room temperature
½ cup melted butter, cooled
2 tablespoons milk, at room temperature
1 teaspoon pure vanilla extract
2 cups all-purpose flour
½ cup sugar
1¼ teaspoons baking powder
½ teaspoon baking soda
½ teaspoon salt
½ cup peanut butter chips
½ cup semisweet chocolate chips
Directions:
Stir together the bananas, eggs, butter, milk, and vanilla in the

bread machine bucket and set it aside.

In a medium bowl, toss together the flour, sugar, baking powder, baking soda, salt, peanut butter chips, and chocolate chips.

Add the dry ingredients to the bucket.

Program the machine for Quick/Rapid bread, and press Start.

When the loaf is done, stick a knife into it, and if it comes out clean, the loaf is done.

If the loaf needs a few more minutes, check the control panel for a Bake Only button and extend the time by 10 minutes.

When the loaf is done, remove the bucket from the machine.

Let the loaf cool for 5 minutes.

Gently shake the bucket to remove the loaf, and turn it out onto a rack to cool.

Nutrition:
Calories: 297
Total Fat : 14g
Saturated Fat: 7g
Carbohydrates: 40g
fiber: 1g
Sodium: 255mg
Protein: 4g

Chocolate Sour Cream Bread

Preparation Time: 20 minutes
Cooking Time: 30-45 minutes
Servings: Makes 1 loaf
Ingredients:

12 SLICES / 1½ TO 2 POUNDS
1 cup sour cream
2 eggs, at room temperature
1 cup sugar
½ cup (1 stick) butter, at room temperature
¼ cup plain Greek yogurt
1¾ cups all-purpose flour
½ cup unsweetened cocoa powder
½ teaspoon baking powder
½ teaspoon salt
1 cup milk chocolate chips

Directions:

In a small bowl, whisk together the sour cream, eggs, sugar, butter, and yogurt until just combined.

Transfer the wet ingredients to the bread machine bucket, and then add the flour, cocoa powder, baking powder, salt, and chocolate chips.

Program the machine for Quick/Rapid bread, and press Start.

When the loaf is done, stick a knife into it, and if it comes out clean, the loaf is done.

If the loaf needs a few more minutes, check the control panel for a Bake Only button and extend the time by 10 minutes.

When the loaf is done, remove the bucket from the machine.

Let the loaf cool for 5 minutes.

Gently shake the bucket to remove the loaf, and turn it out onto a rack to cool.

Nutrition:
Calories: 347

Total Fat : 16g
Saturated Fat: 9g
Carbohydrates: 48g
fiber: 2g
Sodium: 249mg
Protein: 6g

Christmas Fruit Bread

Preparation Time: 10 minutes
Cooking Time: 20-30 minutes
Servings: Makes 1 loaf
Ingredients:
8 SLICES / 1 POUND
¾ cup plus 1 tablespoon milk, at 80°F to 90°F
2⅔ tablespoons melted butter, cooled
⅓ teaspoon pure vanilla extract
⅛ teaspoon pure almond extract
2 tablespoons light brown sugar
⅔ teaspoon salt
1 teaspoon ground cinnamon
2 cups white bread flour
⅔ teaspoon bread machine or instant yeast
⅓ cup dried mixed fruit
⅓ cup golden raisins
12 SLICES / 1½ POUNDS
1¼ cups milk, at 80°F to 90°F
¼ cup melted butter, cooled
½ teaspoon pure vanilla extract
¼ teaspoon pure almond extract
3 tablespoons light brown sugar
1 teaspoon salt
2 teaspoons ground cinnamon

3 cups white bread flour
1 teaspoon bread machine or instant yeast
½ cup dried mixed fruit
½ cup golden raisins
16 SLICES / 2 POUNDS
1⅔ cups milk, at 80°F to 90°F
⅓ cup melted butter, cooled
⅔ teaspoon pure vanilla extract
¼ teaspoon pure almond extract
⅓ cup light brown sugar
1⅓ teaspoons salt
2 teaspoons ground cinnamon
4 cups white bread flour
1⅔ teaspoons bread machine or instant yeast
⅔ cup dried mixed fruit
⅔ cup golden raisins

Directions:
Place the ingredients, except the dried fruit and raisins, in your bread machine as recommended by the manufacturer.
Program the machine for Basic/White bread, select light or medium crust, and press Start.
Add the dried fruit and raisins when the machine signals or 5 minutes before the second kneading cycle is finished.
When the loaf is done, remove the bucket from the machine.
Let the loaf cool for 5 minutes.
Gently shake the bucket to remove the loaf, and turn it out onto a rack to cool.
Nutrition:

Calories: 200
Total Fat: 5g
Saturated Fat: 3g
Carbohydrates: 35g
fiber: 2g
Sodium: 235mg
Protein: 5g

Panettone Bread

Preparation Time: 10 minutes
Cooking Time: 20-30 minutes
Servings: Makes 1 loaf
Ingredients:
8 SLICES / 1 POUND
½ cup milk, at 80°F to 90°F
3 tablespoons melted butter, cooled
1 egg, at room temperature
1⅓ teaspoons pure vanilla extract
4 teaspoons sugar
1 teaspoon salt
2 cups plus 2 tablespoons white bread flour
1½ teaspoons bread machine or instant yeast
3 tablespoons candied lemon peel
3 tablespoons candied orange peel
12 SLICES / 1½ POUNDS
¾ cup milk, at 80°F to 90°F
¼ cup melted butter, cooled
2 eggs, at room temperature
2 teaspoons pure vanilla extract
2 tablespoons sugar
1½ teaspoons salt
3¼ cups white bread flour
2 teaspoons bread machine or instant yeast
¼ cup candied lemon peel
¼ cup candied orange peel

16 SLICES / 2 POUNDS
1 cup milk, at 80°F to 90°F
5 tablespoons melted butter, cooled
3 eggs, at room temperature
2 teaspoons pure vanilla extract
2⅔ tablespoons sugar
2 teaspoons salt
4⅓ cups white bread flour
2¼ teaspoons bread machine or instant yeast
⅓ cup candied lemon peel
⅓ cup candied orange peel
Directions:
Place the ingredients, except the candied fruit peel, in your bread machine as recommended by the manufacturer.
Program the machine for Sweet bread, select light or medium crust, and press Start. When the machine signals, add the peel, or place in the nut/raisin hopper and let the machine add the peel automatically.
When the loaf is done, remove the bucket from the machine. Let the loaf cool for 5 minutes.
Gently shake the bucket to remove the loaf, and turn it out onto a rack to cool.
Nutrition:
Calories: 191
Total Fat : 5g
Saturated Fat: 3g
Carbohydrates: 30g
fiber: 1g
Sodium: 338mg
Protein: 5g

Hot Buttered Rum Bread

Preparation Time: 10 minutes
Cooking Time: 20-30 minutes
Servings: Makes 1 loaf
Ingredients:
8 SLICES / 1 POUND
½ cup minus 1 tablespoon water, at 80°F to 90°F
1 egg, at room temperature
2 tablespoons butter, melted and cooled
2 tablespoons sugar
2 teaspoons rum extract
¾ teaspoon salt
⅔ teaspoon ground cinnamon
¼ teaspoon ground nutmeg
2 cups white bread flour
⅓ teaspoon bread machine or instant yeast
12 SLICES / 1½ POUNDS
¾ cup water, at 80°F to 90°F
1 egg, at room temperature
3 tablespoons butter, melted and cooled
3 tablespoons sugar
1 tablespoon rum extract
1¼ teaspoons salt
1 teaspoon ground cinnamon
¼ teaspoon ground nutmeg
3 cups white bread flour
1 teaspoon bread machine or instant yeast
16 SLICES / 2 POUNDS
1 cup plus 2 tablespoons water, at 80°F to 90°F
1 egg, at room temperature
¼ cup butter, melted and cooled
¼ cup sugar
4 teaspoons rum extract
1⅔ teaspoons salt
1⅓ teaspoons ground cinnamon
¼ teaspoon ground nutmeg
4 cups white bread flour
1⅓ teaspoons bread machine or instant yeast
Directions:
Place the ingredients in your bread machine as recommended by the manufacturer.
Program the machine for Sweet bread and press Start. When the loaf is done, remove the bucket from the machine. Let the loaf cool for 5 minutes.
Gently shake the bucket to remove the loaf, and turn it out onto a rack to cool.
Nutrition:
Calories: 161
Total Fat : 4g
Saturated Fat: 2g
Carbohydrates: 27g
fiber: 1g
Sodium: 271mg
Protein: 4g

Honey-Flavored Bread

Preparation Time: 30-45 minutes

Cooking Time: 30-45 minutes
Servings: Makes 1 loaf
Ingredients:
2¼ cups white flour
¼ cup rye flour
1 cup water
1 whole egg, beaten
1 tablespoon vegetable oil
1 teaspoon salt
1½ tablespoons honey
1 teaspoon dry yeast
Directions:
Add all of the ingredients to your bread machine, carefully following the instructions of the manufacturer.
Set the program of your bread machine to Basic/White Bread and set crust type to Medium. Press START.
Wait until the cycle completes. Once the loaf is ready, take the bucket out and let the loaf cool for 5 minutes.
Gently shake the bucket to remove the loaf.
Transfer to a cooling rack, slice, and serve.
Nutrition: Total Carbs: 33g, Fiber: 1g
protein: 6g
fat: 3g,
Calories: 177

Delicious Honey Lavender Bread

Preparation Time: 30-45 minutes
Cooking Time: 30-45 minutes
Servings: Makes 1 loaf
Ingredients:
1½ cups wheat flour

2⅓ cups whole meal flour
1 teaspoon fresh yeast
1½ cups water
1 teaspoon lavender
1½ tablespoons honey
1 teaspoon salt
Directions:
Sift both types of flour in a bowl and mix.
Add all of the ingredients to your bread machine, carefully following the instructions of the manufacturer.
Set the program of your bread machine to Basic/White Bread and set crust type to Medium. Press START.
Wait until the cycle completes. Once the loaf is ready, take the bucket out and let the loaf cool for 5 minutes.
Gently shake the bucket to remove the loaf.
Transfer to a cooling rack, slice, and serve.
Nutrition: Total Carbs: 46g, Fiber: 1g
protein: 7.5g
fat: 1.5g,
Calories: 226

Delicious Flax Honey Loaf

Preparation Time: 30-45 minutes
Cooking Time: 30-45 minutes
Servings: Makes 1 loaf

Ingredients:
¾ cup milk, at room temperature
1 tablespoon melted butter
1 tablespoon honey
¾ teaspoon salt
2 tablespoons flaxseeds
2 cups white bread flour
¾ teaspoon bread machine yeast

Directions:
Add all of the ingredients to your bread machine, carefully following the instructions of the manufacturer.
Set the program of your bread machine to Basic/White Bread and set crust type to Medium. Press START.
Wait until the cycle completes.
Once the loaf is ready, take the bucket out and let the loaf cool for 5 minutes.
Gently shake the bucket to remove the loaf.
Transfer to a cooling rack, slice, and serve.
Enjoy!
Nutrition: Total Carbs: 28g, Fiber: 1g protein: 6g fat: 3g, Calories: 158

Raisin Bran Bread

Preparation Time: 10 minutes
Cooking Time: 20-25 minutes
Servings: Makes 1 loaf

Ingredients:
8 SLICES / 1 POUND
¾ cup milk, at 80°F to 90°F
1½ tablespoons melted butter, cooled
2 tablespoons sugar
1 teaspoon salt
¼ cup wheat bran
1¾ cups white bread flour
1 teaspoon bread machine or instant yeast
½ cup raisins
12 SLICES / 1½ POUNDS
1⅛ cup milk, at 80°F to 90°F
2¼ tablespoons melted butter, cooled
3 tablespoons sugar
1½ teaspoons salt
⅓ cup wheat bran
2⅔ cups white bread flour
1½ teaspoons bread machine or instant yeast
¾ cup raisins
16 SLICES / 2 POUNDS
1½ cups milk, at 80°F to 90°F
3 tablespoons melted butter, cooled
¼ cup sugar
2 teaspoons salt
½ cup wheat bran
3½ cups white bread flour
2 teaspoons bread machine or instant yeast
1 cup raisins

Directions:
Place the ingredients, except the raisins, in your bread machine as recommended by the manufacturer.
Program the machine for Basic/White bread, select light or medium crust, and press Start.

When the machine signals, add the raisins, or put them in the nut/raisin hopper and let your machine add them automatically.
When the loaf is done, remove the bucket from the machine. Let the loaf cool for 5 minutes.
Gently shake the bucket to remove the loaf, and turn it out onto a rack to cool.
Nutrition:
Calories: 173
Total Fat: 3g
Saturated Fat: 2g
Carbohydrates: 34g
fiber: 2g
Sodium: 317mg
Protein: 4g

Oat Bran Molasses Bread

Preparation Time: 10 minutes
Cooking Time: 20-30 minutes
Servings: Makes 1 loaf
Ingredients:
8 SLICES / 1 POUND
½ cup water, at 80°F to 90°F
1½ tablespoons melted butter, cooled
2 tablespoons blackstrap molasses
¼ teaspoon salt
⅛ teaspoon ground nutmeg
½ cup oat bran
1½ cups whole-wheat bread flour
1⅛ teaspoons bread machine or instant yeast
12 SLICES / 1½ POUNDS
¾ cup water, at 80°F to 90°F
2¼ tablespoons melted butter, cooled
3 tablespoons blackstrap molasses
⅓ teaspoon salt
¼ teaspoon ground nutmeg
¾ cup oat bran
2¼ cups whole-wheat bread flour
1⅔ teaspoons bread machine or instant yeast
16 SLICES / 2 POUNDS
1 cup water, at 80°F to 90°F
3 tablespoons melted butter, cooled
¼ cup blackstrap molasses
½ teaspoon salt
¼ teaspoon ground nutmeg
1 cup oat bran
3 cups whole-wheat bread flour
2¼ teaspoons bread machine or instant yeast
Directions:
Place the ingredients in your bread machine as recommended by the manufacturer.
Program the machine for Whole-Wheat/Whole-Grain bread, select light or medium crust, and press Start.

When the loaf is done, remove the bucket from the machine. Let the loaf cool for 5 minutes.
Gently shake the bucket to remove the loaf, and turn it out onto a rack to cool.
Nutrition:
Calories: 137
Total Fat : 3g
Saturated Fat: 2g
Carbohydrates: 25g
fiber: 1g
Sodium: 112mg
Protein: 3g

Bran Bread

Preparation Time: 30-45 minutes
Cooking Time: 30-45 minutes
Servings: Makes 1 loaf
Ingredients:
2 ½ cups (320 g) all-purpose flour, sifted
1 whole egg
¾ cup (40 g) bran
1 cup (240 ml) lukewarm water
1 tablespoon sunflower oil
2 teaspoons brown sugar
1 teaspoon sea salt
1 teaspoon active dry yeast
Directions:
Prepare all of the ingredients for your bread and measuring means (a cup, a spoon, kitchen scales).
Carefully measure the ingredients into the pan. Place all of the ingredients into the bread bucket in the right order, following the manual for your bread machine.

Close the cover.
Select the program of your bread machine to FRENCH BREAD and choose the crust color to MEDIUM.
Press START.
Wait until the program completes.
When done, take the bucket out and let it cool for 5-10 minutes.
Shake the loaf from the pan and let cool for 30 minutes on a cooling rack.
Slice, serve and enjoy the taste of fragrant homemade bread.
Nutrition:
Calories 307
Total Fat 5.1g
Saturated Fat 0.9g
Cholesterol 33g
Sodium 480mg
Total Carbohydrate 54g
Dietary Fiber 7.9g
Total Sugars 1.8g
Protein 10.2g

Whole-Wheat Challah

Preparation Time: 10 minutes
Cooking Time: 20-30 minutes
Servings: Makes 1 loaf

Ingredients:
8 SLICES / 1 POUND
½ cup water, at 80°F to 90°F
¼ cup melted butter, cooled
1 egg, at room temperature
1 teaspoon salt
2 tablespoons sugar
¾ cup whole-wheat flour
1¼ cups white bread flour
1⅛ teaspoons bread machine
or instant yeast
12 SLICES / 1½ POUNDS
¾ cup water, at 80°F to 90°F
⅓ cup melted butter, cooled
2 eggs, at room temperature
1½ teaspoons salt
3 tablespoons sugar
1 cup whole-wheat flour
2 cups white bread flour
1⅔ teaspoons bread machine
or instant yeast
16 SLICES / 2 POUNDS
1 cup water, at 80°F to 90°F
½ cup melted butter, cooled
2 eggs, at room temperature
2 teaspoons salt
¼ cup sugar
1½ cups whole-wheat flour
2½ cups white bread flour
2¼ teaspoons bread machine
or instant yeast
Directions:
Place the ingredients in your
bread machine as
recommended by the
manufacturer.
Program the machine for
Basic/White bread, select light
or medium crust, and press
Start.
When the loaf is done, remove
the bucket from the machine.

Let the loaf cool for 5
minutes.
Gently shake the bucket to
remove the loaf, and turn it
out onto a rack to cool.
Nutrition:
Calories: 183
Total Fat: 6g
Saturated Fat: 4g
Carbohydrates: 27g fiber: 1g
Sodium: 339mg
Protein: 5g

Whole-Wheat Sourdough Bread

Preparation Time: 10 minutes
Cooking Time: 20-30 minutes
Servings: Makes 1 loaf
Ingredients:
8 SLICES / 1 POUND
⅔ cups water, at 80°F to 90°F
⅔ cup No-Yeast Whole-Wheat Sourdough Starter (here), fed, active, and at room temperature
4 teaspoons melted butter, cooled
2 teaspoons sugar
1 teaspoon salt
2 cups whole-wheat flour
1¼ teaspoons bread machine or instant yeast
12 SLICES / 1½ POUNDS
¾ cup plus 2 tablespoons water, at 80°F to 90°F
¾ cup plus 2 tablespoons No-Yeast Whole-Wheat Sourdough Starter (here), fed, active, and at room temperature
2 tablespoons melted butter, cooled
1 tablespoon sugar
1½ teaspoons salt
3 cups whole-wheat flour
1¾ teaspoons bread machine or instant yeast
16 SLICES / 2 POUNDS
1¼ cups water, at 80°F to 90°F
1¼ cups No-Yeast Whole-Wheat Sourdough Starter (here), fed, active, and at room temperature
2⅔ tablespoons melted butter, cooled
4 teaspoons sugar

2 teaspoons salt
4 cups whole-wheat flour
2½ teaspoons bread machine or instant yeast
Directions:
Place the ingredients in your bread machine as recommended by the manufacturer.
Program the machine for Whole-Wheat/Whole-Grain bread, select light or medium crust, and press Start.
When the loaf is done, remove the bucket from the machine.
Let the loaf cool for 5 minutes.
Gently shake the bucket to remove the loaf, and turn it out onto a rack to cool.
Nutrition:
Calories: 155
Total Fat : 2g
Saturated Fat: 1g
Carbohydrates: 29g
fiber: 1g
Sodium: 305mg
Protein: 4g

Faithful Italian Semolina Bread

Preparation Time: 30-45 minutes
Cooking Time: 30-45 minutes
Servings: Makes 1 loaf
Ingredients:
1 cup water
1 teaspoon salt
2½ tablespoons butter
2½ teaspoons sugar
2¼ cups flour
⅓ cups semolina
1½ teaspoons dry yeast

Directions:
Add all of the ingredients to your bread machine, carefully following the instructions of the manufacturer.
Set the program of your bread machine to Italian Bread/Sandwich mode and set crust type to Medium.
Press START.
Wait until the cycle completes. Once the loaf is ready, take the bucket out and let the loaf cool for 5 minutes.
Gently shake the bucket to remove the loaf.
Transfer to a cooling rack, slice, and serve.
Nutrition: Total Carbs: 45g, Fiber: 1g
protein: 7g
fat: 10g,
Calories: 302

Mediterranean Semolina Bread

Preparation Time: 30-45 minutes
Cooking Time: 3 ½ hours
Servings: Makes 1 loaf
Ingredients:
1 cup lukewarm water (80 degrees F)
1 teaspoon salt
2½ tablespoons butter, melted
2½ teaspoons white sugar
2¼ cups all-purpose flour
⅓ cups semolina
1½ teaspoons active dry yeast
Directions:
Prepare all of the ingredients for your bread and measuring means (a cup, a spoon, kitchen scales).
Carefully measure the ingredients into the pan.
Place all of the ingredients into the bread bucket in the right order, following the manual for your bread machine.
Close the cover.
Select the program of your bread machine to ITALIAN BREAD / SANDWICH mode and choose the crust color to MEDIUM.
Press START.
Wait until the program completes.
When done, take the bucket out and let it cool for 5-10 minutes.
Shake the loaf from the pan and let cool for 30 minutes on a cooling rack.
Slice and serve.
Nutrition:
Calories 243
Total Fat 8.1g
Saturated Fat 4.9g
Cholesterol 20g
Sodium 203mg
Total Carbohydrate 37g
Dietary Fiber 1.5g
Total Sugars 2.8g
Protein 5.3g, Vitamin D 5mcg,
Calcium 10mg, Iron 2mg,
Potassium 80mg

Multigrain Sourdough Bread

Preparation Time: 10 minutes
Cooking Time: 20-30 minutes
Servings: Makes 1 loaf

Ingredients:
8 SLICES / 1 POUND
⅓ cup plus 1 tablespoon water, at 80°F to 90°F
½ cup Simple Sourdough Starter (here), fed, active, and at room temperature
4 teaspoons melted butter, cooled
1⅔ tablespoons sugar
½ teaspoon salt
½ cup multigrain cereal (Bob's Red Mill or equivalent)
1¾ cups white bread flour
1 teaspoon bread machine or instant yeast
12 SLICES / 1½ POUNDS
⅔ cup water, at 80°F to 90°F
¾ cup Simple Sourdough Starter (here), fed, active, and at room temperature
2 tablespoons melted butter, cooled
2½ tablespoons sugar
¾ teaspoon salt
¾ cup multigrain cereal (Bob's Red Mill or equivalent)
2⅔ cups white bread flour
1½ teaspoons bread machine or instant yeast
16 SLICES / 2 POUNDS
¾ cup plus 1 tablespoon water, at 80°F to 90°F
1 cup Simple Sourdough Starter (here), fed, active, and at room temperature
2⅔ tablespoons melted butter, cooled
3⅓ tablespoons sugar
1 teaspoon salt
1 cup multigrain cereal (Bob's Red Mill or equivalent)
3½ cups white bread flour

2 teaspoons bread machine or instant yeast
Directions:
Place the ingredients in your bread machine as recommended by the manufacturer.
Program the machine for Whole-Wheat/Whole-Grain bread, select light or medium crust, and press Start.
When the loaf is done, remove the bucket from the machine. Let the loaf cool for 5 minutes.
Gently shake the bucket to remove the loaf, and turn it out onto a rack to cool.
Nutrition:
Calories: 172
Total Fat: 2g
Saturated Fat: 1g
Carbohydrates: 32g
fiber: 2g
Sodium: 162mg
Protein: 14g

Awesome Multigrain Bread

Preparation Time: 30-45 minutes
Cooking Time: 30-45 minutes

Servings: Makes 1 loaf
Ingredients:
¾ cup water at 80 degrees F
1 tablespoon melted butter
½ tablespoon honey
½ teaspoon salt
¾ cup multigrain flour
1⅓ cups white bread flour
1 teaspoon active dry yeast
Directions:
Add all of the ingredients to
your bread machine, carefully
following the instructions of
the manufacturer.
Set the program of your bread
machine to Basic/White Bread
and set crust type to Medium.
Press START.
Wait until the cycle completes.
Once the loaf is ready, take the
bucket out and let the loaf
cool for 5 minutes.
Gently shake the bucket to
remove the loaf.
Transfer to a cooling rack,
slice, and serve.
Nutrition: Total Carbs: 27g,
Fiber: 2g
protein: 4g
fat: 2g,
Calories: 145

Multigrain Bread

Preparation Time: 30 minutes
Cooking Time: 2-3 hours
Servings: Makes 1 loaf

Ingredients:

¾ cup lukewarm water (80 degrees F)
1 tablespoon melted butter
½ tablespoon liquid honey
½ teaspoon salt
¾ cup multigrain flour
1⅓ cups wheat flour
1 teaspoon active dry yeast

Directions:

Prepare all of the ingredients for your bread and measuring means (a cup, a spoon, kitchen scales).

Carefully measure the ingredients into the pan.

Place all of the ingredients, into the bread bucket in the right order, following the manual for your bread machine.

Close the cover.

Select the program of your bread machine to FRENCH BREAD and choose the crust color to MEDIUM.

Press START.

Wait until the program completes.

When done, take the bucket out and let it cool for 5-10 minutes.

Shake the loaf from the pan and let cool for 30 minutes on a cooling rack.

Slice, serve and enjoy the taste of fragrant homemade bread.

Nutrition:

Calories 124
Total Fat 2.8g
Saturated Fat 1.1g
Cholesterol 4g
Sodium 207mg
Total Carbohydrate 22.8g
Dietary Fiber 3.3g
Total Sugars 1.5g
Protein 4.6g, Vitamin D 1mcg,
Calcium 12mg, Iron 1mg,
Potassium 33mg

Chapter 15 Keto Breads

Keto Breakfast Bread

Preparation Time: 15 minutes
Cooking Time: 40 minutes
Servings: 16 slices
Ingredients:
½ tsp. xanthan gum
½ tsp. salt
2 Tbsp. coconut oil
½ cup butter, melted
1 tsp. baking powder
2 cups of almond flour
7 eggs
Directions:
Preheat the oven to 355F.
Beat eggs in a bowl on high for 2 minutes.
Add coconut oil and butter to the eggs and continue to beat.
Line a loaf pan with baking paper and pour the beaten eggs.
Pour in the rest of the ingredients and mix until it becomes thick.
Bake until a toothpick comes out dry, about 40 to 45 minutes.
Nutrition:
Calories: 234
Fat: 23g
Carb: 1g
Protein: 7g

Chia Seed Bread

Preparation Time: 10 minutes
Cooking Time: 40 minutes
Servings: 16 slices
Ingredients:
½ tsp. xanthan gum
½ cup butter
2 Tbsp. coconut oil
1 Tbsp. baking powder
3 Tbsp. sesame seeds
2 Tbsp. chia seeds
½ tsp. salt
¼ cup sunflower seeds
2 cups almond flour   7 eggs
Directions:
Preheat the oven to 350F.
Beat eggs in a bowl on high for 1 to 2 minutes.
Beat in the xanthan gum and combine coconut oil and melted butter into eggs, beating continuously.
Set aside the sesame seeds, but add the rest of the ingredients.
Line a loaf pan with baking paper and place the mixture in it. Top the mixture with sesame seeds.
Bake in the oven until a toothpick inserted comes out clean, about 35 to 40 minutes.
Nutrition:
Calories: 405   Fat: 37g
Carb: 4g   Protein: 14g

Keto Flax Bread

Preparation Time: 10 minutes
Cooking Time: 18 to 20 minutes
Servings: 8
Ingredients:
¾ cup of water
200 g ground flax seeds
½ cup psyllium husk powder
1 Tbsp. baking powder
7 large egg whites
3 Tbsp. butter

2 tsp. salt
¼ cup granulated stevia
1 large whole egg
1 ½ cups whey protein isolate
Directions:
Preheat the oven to 350F.
Combine together whey protein isolate, psyllium husk, baking powder, sweetener, and salt.
In another bowl, mix together the water, butter, egg, and egg whites.
Slowly add psyllium husk mixture to egg mixture and mix well.
Lightly grease a bread pan with butter and pour in the batter.
Bake in the oven until the bread is set, about 18 to 20 minutes.
Nutrition:
Calories: 265.5
Fat: 15.68g
Carb: 1.88g
Protein:24.34 g

Special Keto Bread

Preparation Time: 15 minutes
Cooking Time: 40 minutes
Servings: 14
Ingredients:
2 tsp. baking powder
½ cup water
1 Tbsp. poppy seeds
2 cups fine ground almond meal
5 large eggs
½ cup olive oil
½ tsp. fine Himalayan salt
Directions:
Preheat the oven to 400F.

In a bowl, combine salt, almond meal, and baking powder.
Drip in oil while mixing, until it forms a crumbly dough.
Make a little round hole in the middle of the dough and pour eggs into the middle of the dough.
Pour water and whisk eggs together with the mixer in the small circle until it is frothy.
Start making larger circles to combine the almond meal mixture with the dough until you have a smooth and thick batter.
Line your loaf pan with parchment paper.
Pour batter into the prepared loaf pan and sprinkle poppy seeds on top.
Bake in the oven for 40 minutes in the center rack until firm and golden brown.
Cool in the oven for 30 minutes.
Slice and serve.
Nutrition:
Calories: 227
Fat: 21g
Carb: 4g
Protein: 7g

Keto Easy Bread

Preparation Time: 15 minutes
Cooking Time: 45 minutes
Servings: 10
Ingredients:
¼ tsp. cream of tartar
1 ½ tsp. baking powder (double acting)
4 large eggs

1 ½ cups vanilla whey protein
¼ cup olive oil
¼ cup coconut milk, unsweetened
½ tsp. salt
¼ cup unsalted butter, softened
12 oz. cream cheese, softened
½ tsp. xanthan gum
½ tsp. baking soda

Directions:
Preheat oven to 325F.
Layer aluminum foil over the loaf pan and spray with olive oil.
Beat the butter with cream cheese in a bowl until mixed well.
Add oil and coconut milk and blend until mixed. Add eggs, one by one until fully mixed. Set aside.
In a bowl, whisk whey protein, ½ tsp. xanthan gum, baking soda, cream of tartar, salt, and baking powder.
Add mixture to egg/cheese mixture and slowly mix until fully combined. Don't over blend.
Place in the oven and bake for 40 to 45 minutes, or until golden brown.
Cool, slice, and serve.
Nutrition:
Calories: 294.2
Fat: 24g
Carb: 1.8g
Protein: 17g

Low Carb Bread

Preparation Time: 10 minutes
Cooking Time: 21 minutes

Servings: 12
Ingredients:
2 cups mozzarella cheese, grated
8 oz. cream cheese
herbs and spices to taste
1 Tbsp. baking powder
1 cup crushed pork rinds
¼ cup parmesan cheese, grated
3 large eggs

Directions:
Preheat oven to 375F.
Line parchment paper over the baking pan.
In a bowl, place cream cheese and mozzarella and microwave for 1 minute on high power. Stir and microwave for 1 minute more. Then stir again. Stir in egg, parmesan, pork rinds, herbs, spices and baking powder until mixed.
Spread mixture on the baking pan and bake until top is lightly brown, about 15 to 20 minutes.
Cool, slice, and serve.
Nutrition:
Calories: 166
Fat: 13g
Carb: 1g
Protein: 9g

Splendid Low-Carb Bread

Preparation Time: 15 minutes
Cooking Time: 60 to 70 minutes
Servings: 12
Ingredients:
½ tsp. herbs, such as basil, rosemary, or oregano

½ tsp. garlic or onion powder
1 Tbsp. baking powder
5 Tbsp. psyllium husk powder
½ cup almond flour
½ cup coconut flour
¼ tsp. salt
1 ½ cup egg whites
3 Tbsp. oil or melted butter
2 Tbsp. apple cider vinegar
1/3 to ¾ cup hot water

Directions:
Grease a loaf pan and preheat the oven to 350F.
In a bowl, whisk the salt, psyllium husk powder, onion or garlic powder, coconut flour, almond flour, and baking powder.
Stir in egg whites, oil, and apple cider vinegar. Bit by bit add the hot water, stirring until dough increase in size.
Do not add too much water.
Mold the dough into a rectangle and transfer to grease loaf pan.
Bake in the oven for 60 to 70 minutes, or until crust feels firm and brown on top.
Cool and serve.
Nutrition:
Calories: 97
Fat: 5.7g
Carb: 7.5g
Protein: 4.1g

Bread De Soul

Preparation Time: 10 minutes
Cooking Time: 45 minutes
Servings: 16

Ingredients:
¼ tsp. cream of tartar
2 ½ tsp. baking powder

1 tsp. xanthan gum
1/3 tsp. baking soda
½ tsp. salt
1 2/3 cup unflavored whey protein
¼ cup olive oil
¼ cup heavy whipping cream or half and half
2 drops of sweet leaf stevia
4 eggs
¼ cup butter
12 oz. softened cream cheese

Directions:
Preheat the oven to 325F.
In a bowl, microwave cream cheese and butter for 1 minute.
Remove and blend well with a hand mixer.
Add olive oil, eggs, heavy cream, and few drops of sweetener and blend well.
Blend together the dry ingredients in a separate bowl.
Combine the dry ingredients with the wet ingredients and mix with a spoon. Don't use a hand blender to avoid whipping it too much.
Grease a bread pan and pour the mixture into the pan.
Bake in the oven until golden brown, about 45 minutes.
Cool and serve.
Nutrition:
Calories: 200
Fat: 15.2g
Carb: 1.8g
Protein: 10g

Sandwich Flatbread

Preparation Time: 15 minutes
Cooking Time: 20 minutes

Servings: 10
Ingredients: ¼ cup water
¼ cup oil   4 eggs
½ tsp. salt
1/3 cup unflavored whey
protein powder
½ tsp. garlic powder
2 tsp. baking powder
6 Tbsp. coconut flour
3 ¼ cups almond flour
Directions: Preheat the oven
to 325F. Combine the dry
ingredients in a large bowl
and mix with a hand whisk.
Whisk in eggs, oil, and water
until combined well.
Place on a piece of large
parchment paper and flatten
into a rough rectangle. Place
another parchment paper on
top.
Roll into a large ½ inch to ¾
inch thick rough rectangle.
Transfer to the baking sheet
and discard the parchment
paper on top.
Bake until it is firm to the
touch, about 20 minutes.
Cool and cut into 10
portions.
Carefully cut each part into
two halves through the bready
center. Stuff with your
sandwich fillings.   Serve.
Nutrition: Calories: 316
Fat: 6.8g   Carb: 11g
Protein: 25.9g

Keto Sandwich Bread

Preparation Time: 5 minutes
Cooking Time: 1 hour
Servings: 12
Ingredients:

1 tsp. apple cider vinegar
¾ cup water
¼ cup avocado oil
5 eggs
½ tsp. salt
1 tsp. baking soda
½ cup coconut flour
2 cups plus 2 Tbsp. almond
flour
Directions:
Preheat the oven to 350F and
grease a loaf pan.
In a bowl, whisk almond flour,
coconut flour, and salt.
In another bowl, separate the
egg whites from egg yolks. Set
egg whites aside.
In a blender, blend the oil, egg
yolks, water, vinegar, and
baking soda for 5 minutes on
medium speed until
combined.
Let the mixture sit for 1
minute then add in the
reserved egg whites and mix
until frothy, about 10 to 15
seconds.
Add the dry ingredients and
process on high for 5 to 10
seconds before batter becomes
too thick for the blender.
Blend until the batter is
smooth.
Transfer batter into the
greased loaf pan and
smoothen the top.
Bake in the oven until a
skewer inserted comes out
clean, about 50 to 70 minutes.
Cool, slice, and serve.
Nutrition:
Calories: 200g
Fat: 7g
Carb: 7g

Protein: 16g

Easy Bake Keto Bread

Preparation Time: 10 minutes
Cooking Time: 30 minutes
Servings: 16
Ingredients:
7 whole eggs
4.5 oz. melted butter
2 Tbsp. warm water
2 tsp dry yeast
1 tsp. inulin
1 pinch of salt
1 tsp. xanthan gum
1 tsp. baking powder
1 Tbsp. psyllium husk powder
2 cups almond flour
Directions:
Preheat the oven to 340F.
In a bowl, mix almond flour, salt, psyllium, baking powder, and xanthan gum.
Make a well in the center of the mixture.
Add the yeast and inulin into the center with the warm water.
Stir the inulin and yeast with the warm water in the center and let the yeast activate, about 10 minutes.
Add in the eggs and melted butter and stir well.
Pour the mixture into a loaf pan lined with parchment paper.
Allow batter to proof in a warm spot covered for 20 minutes with a tea towel.
Place in the oven and bake until golden brown, about 30 to 40 minutes.

Cool, slice, and serve.
Nutrition:
Calories: 140
Fat: 13g
Carb: 3g
Protein: 3g

Keto Bakers Bread

Preparation Time: 10 minutes
Cooking Time: 20 minutes
Servings: 12
Ingredients:
Pinch of salt
4 Tbsp. light cream cheese, softened
½ tsp. cream of tartar
4 eggs, yolks, and whites separated
Directions:
Heat 2 racks in the middle of the oven at 350F.
Line 2 baking pan with parchment paper, then grease with cooking spray.
Separate egg yolks from the whites and place in separate mixing bowls.
Beat the egg whites and cream of tartar with a hand mixer until stiff, about 3 to 5 minutes. Do not over-beat.
Whisk the cream cheese, salt, and egg yolks until smooth.
Slowly fold the cheese mix into the whites until fluffy.
Spoon ¼ cup measure of the batter onto the baking sheets, 6 mounds on each sheet.
Bake in the oven for 20 to 22 minutes, alternating racks halfway through.
Cool and serve.
Nutrition:

Calories: 41
Fat: 3.2g
Carb: 1g
Protein: 2.4g

Keto Cloud Bread Cheese

Preparation Time: 5 minutes
Cooking Time: 30 minutes
Servings: 12
Ingredients for cream cheese filling:
1 egg yolk
½ tsp. vanilla stevia drops for filling
8 oz. softened cream cheese
Base egg dough:
½ tsp. cream of tartar
1 Tbsp. coconut flour
¼ cup unflavored whey protein
3 oz. softened cream cheese
¼ tsp. vanilla stevia drops for dough
4 eggs, separated
Directions:
Preheat the oven to 325F.
Line two baking sheets with parchment paper.
In a bowl, stir the 8 ounces cream cheese, stevia, and egg yolk.
Transfer to the pastry bag.
In another bowl, separate egg yolks from whites.
Add 3 oz. cream cheese, yolks, stevia, whey protein, and coconut flour. Mix until smooth.
Whip cream of tartar with the egg whites until stiff peaks form.

Fold in the yolk/cream cheese mixture into the beaten whites.
Spoon batter onto each baking sheet, 6 mounds on each. Press each mound to flatten a bit.
Add cream cheese filling in the middle of each batter.
Bake for 30 minutes at 325F.
Nutrition:
Calories: 120
Fat: 10.7g
Carb: 1.1g
Protein: 5.4g

My Keto Bread

Preparation Time: 10 minutes
Cooking Time: 50 to 60 minutes
Servings: 6
Ingredients:
3 egg whites
1 cup of boiling water

187

2 Tbsp. sesame seeds
2 tsp. cider vinegar
1 tsp. sea salt
2 tsp. baking powder
5 Tbsp. ground psyllium husk powder
1 ¼ cups almond flour

Directions:
Preheat the oven to 350F.
Mix the dry ingredients in a bowl.
In another bowl, add the boiling water, vinegar, and egg whites. Beat for 30 seconds with a hand mixer. Don't over mix.
Grease hands with oil to make 6 pieces then arrange on a greased baking sheet.
Bake 50 to 60 minutes in the lower rack of the oven.
Cooking time depends on the size of the bread. The bread is ready when it makes a hollow sound when tapped.
Nutrition:
Calories: 170
Fat: 13g
Carb: 2g
Protein: 7g

Keto Oat Cornbread
Preparation Time: 10 minutes
Cooking Time: 20 minutes
Servings: 8
Ingredients:
¼ tsp. corn extract
4 eggs
¼ cup water
1/3 cup melted bacon fat or coconut oil
4 oz. melted butter
¼ tsp. salt

1 ½ tsp. baking powder
1/3 cup whey protein isolate, unflavored
½ cup oat fiber
¼ cup coconut flour

Directions:
Preheat oven to 350F.
Grease a 10-inch cast iron skillet and place in the oven to warm up.
Combine all the dry ingredients in a bowl. Add the eggs, water, melted butter, and bacon fat. Beat with a hand mixer, then mix in corn extract.
Transfer mixture into the heated skillet.
Bake at 350F for 18 to 20 minutes or until firm and top is lightly browned.
Nutrition:
Calories: 240
Fat: 23g
Carb: 1g
Protein: 7g

Blueberry Zucchini Bread
Preparation Time: 30-45 minutes
Cooking Time: 1 hour 30 minutes
Servings: 18
Ingredients:
1 cup blueberries
1 1/2 cup grated zucchini, moisture removed
2 cups almond flour, blanched
2 teaspoons baking powder
1/4 teaspoon sea salt
1 teaspoon vanilla extract, unsweetened

3/4 cup erythritol sweetener
1/2 cup butter, unsalted, softened
1 tablespoon lemon juice
1 tablespoon lemon zest
3 eggs, pastured

Directions:

Switch on the oven, set it to 325 degrees F and let preheat. Meanwhile, place butter and sweetener in a bowl, whisk until fluffy and then beat in eggs, lemon zest and juice, vanilla until combined.

Then beat in flour, salt, baking powder until incorporated, fold in zucchini and berries, and stir until well mixed.

Take a 9 by 5 inches loaf pan, line it with parchment paper, spoon in batter and bake the bread for 1 hour and 10 minutes or until the bread has cooked and an inserted knife into the bread comes out clean.

Then let the bread cool in the pan completely, cut into 18 slices, and serve.

Nutrition:
139 Cal
12 g Fats
4 g Protein
3 g Net Carb
2 g Fiber

Blueberry Bread

Preparation Time: 30-45 minutes
Cooking Time: 1 hour 30 minutes
Servings: 12

Ingredients:

1/2 cup blueberries
2 cups almond flour, blanched
1/2 cup Erythritol sweetener
2 tablespoons coconut flour
1 teaspoon vanilla extract, unsweetened
1 1/2 teaspoon baking powder
3 tablespoons butter, unsalted, softened
5 eggs, pastured
3 tablespoons heavy whipping cream, grass-fed, full-fat

Directions:

Switch on the oven, set it to 350 degrees F and let preheat. Meanwhile, add vanilla in a bowl along with sweetener and eggs, whisk using an immersion blender until frothy, and then whisk in the cream until combined.

Place remaining ingredients in another bowl, except for butter and berries, stir until mixed, then slowly mix into egg mixture until incorporated and fold in berries until combined.

Take a 9 by 5 inches loaf pan, grease it with butter, pour in prepared batter and bake for 45 to 50 minutes or until the bread has cooked and an inserted toothpick into the bread comes out clean.

Let bread cool in its pan for 10 minutes, then take it out to cool completely on a wire rack, cut the bread into 12 slices and serve.

Nutrition:
175 Cal
15 g Fats
6 g Protein

3 g Net Carb
2 g Fiber

Banana Bread

Preparation Time: 30-45
minutes
Cooking Time: 1 hour 30
minutes
Servings: 12

Ingredients:
2 cup almond flour, blanched
1/4 cup coconut flour
1/2 cup walnuts, chopped
1/4 teaspoon sea salt
2 teaspoons baking powder
1/2 cup erythritol sweetener
2 teaspoons cinnamon
2 teaspoons banana extract,
unsweetened
6 tablespoons butter, unsalted,
softened
4 eggs, pastured
1/4 cup almond milk, full-fat,
unsweetened

Directions:
Switch on the oven, set it to
350 degrees F and let preheat.
Meanwhile, place flours, salt,
baking powder, and cinnamon
in a bowl and stir until mixed.
Place butter into another bowl,
add sweetener, beat until fluffy
and then beat in eggs, banana
extract and milk until
combined.
Slowly beat in flour mixture
until incorporated and a
smooth, fold in walnuts and
transfer the batter into a 9 by
5 inches loaf pan, lined with
parchment sheet.
Bake the bread for 1 hour
until the bread has cooked and

an inserted toothpick slides
out clean.
Let bread cool completely into
the pan, then take it out, cut
into 12 pieces, and serve.
Nutrition: 224 Cal
20 g Fats
8 g Protein
2 g Net Carb
4 g Fiber

Pumpkin Bread

Preparation Time: 30-45
minutes
Cooking Time: 1 hour 30
minutes
Servings: 12

Ingredients:
1/2 cup coconut flour
2 cup almond flour, blanched
1/4 teaspoon sea salt
2 teaspoons pumpkin pie spice
1/4 cup pumpkin seeds
2 teaspoons baking powder
3/4 cup erythritol sweetener
1/3 cup avocado oil
3/4 cup pumpkin puree
4 eggs, beaten

Directions:
Switch on the oven, set it to
350 degrees F and let preheat.
Meanwhile, place flours in a
bowl, stir in sweetener, salt,
baking powder, and pumpkin
spice, and then whisk in
butter, eggs and pumpkin
puree until incorporated and a
smooth.
Take a 9 by 5 inches loaf pan,
pour in batter, smooth the
batter from the top, sprinkle
pumpkin seeds on top and
bake for the bread for 1 hour

or until the bread has cooked and an inserted toothpick slides out clean.

Let the bread cool in its pan, then take it out, cut into 12 slices and serve.

Nutrition: 215 Cal

18 g Fats

8 g Protein

4 g Net Carb

5 g Fiber

Cinnamon Butter Loaf

Preparation Time: 30-45 minutes

Cooking Time: 1 hour 30 minutes

Servings: 16

Ingredients:

2 1/2 cups almond flour, blanched

1/4 cup chopped walnuts

4 tablespoons psyllium husk

1/2 teaspoon salt

1 tablespoon and 2 teaspoons cinnamon

1 teaspoon baking powder

1/2 cup erythritol sweetener

1/4 cup avocado oil

1/2 cup hot water

4 eggs, pastured

Directions:

Switch on the oven, set it to 375 degrees F and let preheat. Meanwhile, place flour in a bowl, add husk, salt, sweetener, baking powder, and 1 tablespoon cinnamon until mixed.

Then whisk in hot water, eggs, and oil until combined, take an 8 inches loaf pan, grease it with oil and pour in half of the batter.

Sprinkle with remaining cinnamon, pour in remaining batter, then create patterns into the batter by swirling it with a knife and top with walnuts.

Bake the bread for 40 minutes or until the bread has cooked and an inserted skewer into the pan slides out clean.

Let the bread cool in the pan, then take it out, cut into 16 slices, and serve.

Nutrition:

166 Cal

14 g Fats

5 g Protein

3 g Net Carb

4 g Fiber

Cinnamon Bread

Preparation Time: 30-45 minutes

Cooking Time: 1 hour 30 minutes

Servings: 12

Ingredients:

2 cups almond flour

1 teaspoon baking soda

⅓ cup erythritol sweetener

1 teaspoon baking powder

2 tablespoons cinnamon

2 teaspoons vanilla extract, unsweetened

¼ cup melted butter

3 tablespoons sour cream, full-fat

3 eggs, pastured

Directions

Switch on the oven, set it to 350 degrees F and let preheat.

Meanwhile, place butter and sweetener in a bowl, beat until fluffy, and then beat in cream, vanilla, and eggs until well combined.

Stir together flour, baking soda, baking powder and cinnamon in another bowl, and then slowly beat into egg mixture until smooth and incorporated.

Take a loaf pan, grease it with oil, pour in the batter and bake for 30 to 40 minutes until done and an inserted skewer into the bread slides out clean.

Let the bread cool in the pan, then take it out, cut into 12 slices, and serve.

Nutrition: 200 Cal
18 g Fats
7 g Protein
4 g Net Carb
3 g Fiber

Switch on the oven, set it to 350 degrees F and let preheat. Meanwhile, add nuts in a food processor, blend until nut butter comes together and then blend in eggs, one at a time, until well incorporated. Blend in flour, vinegar, and baking soda until incorporated and then transfer the batter into the loaf pan lined with parchment sheet and bake for 30 to 40 minutes or until the bread has cooked and an inserted skewer into the bread slides out clean.

Let the bread cool in the pan, then take it out, cut into ten slices and serve.

Nutrition: 151 Cal
14 g Fats 5 g Protein
3 g Net Carb 4 g Fiber

Macadamia Nut Bread

Preparation Time: 30-45 minutes
Cooking Time: 1 hour 30 minutes
Servings: 10

Ingredients:
1/4 cup coconut flour
5 ounces macadamia nuts
5 eggs, pastured
1/2 teaspoon baking soda
1/2 teaspoon apple cider vinegar

Directions:

Strawberry Bread

Preparation Time: 30-45 minutes
Cooking Time: 1 hour 30 minutes
Servings: 10

Ingredients:

3/4 cup fresh strawberries, chopped
12 tablespoons coconut flour
1/2 teaspoon salt
1 1/2 teaspoon baking powder
1/2 teaspoon cinnamon
1 1/2 teaspoon vanilla extract, unsweetened
5 eggs, pastured
8 tablespoons melted butter, unsalted
1 egg white, pastured
1 cup erythritol sweetener
2 tablespoons whipping cream, grass-fed, full-fat
2 tablespoons sour cream, full-fat

For the Icing:

1/4 cup fresh strawberries, chopped
1 tablespoon butter, melted, unsalted
3/4 cup erythritol sweetener
2 tablespoons heavy whipping cream, grass-fed

Directions:

Switch on the oven, set it to 350 degrees F and let preheat. Meanwhile, add eggs and egg whites into a bowl, add sour cream, whipping cream, sweetener, salt, baking powder, vanilla, and cinnamon and beat until combined.

Blend in butter until combined, slowly stir in flour and fold in berries until combined.

Take a loaf pan, line it with parchment paper, pour in batter and bake the cake for 1 hour and 10 minutes or until the bread has cooked and an inserted skewer into the bread slides out clean.

Meanwhile, prepare the icing and for this, place all the ingredients in a bowl, whisk until well combined and set aside.

When the bread has baked, let the bread cool in the pan, then take it out, spread the icing on top, cut into ten slices and serve.

Nutrition:

192 Cal
16 g Fats
4 g Protein
3 g Net Carb
3 g Fiber

Nut and Seed Bread

Preparation Time: 30-45 minutes

Cooking Time: 1 hour 30 minutes

Servings: 16

Ingredients:

1/2 cup flax seed
1/2 cup sesame seeds
1/2 cup pistachios
1/2 cup almonds
1/2 cup cashews
1/2 cup walnuts
1/3 tsp salt
1/4 cup avocado oil
3 eggs, pastured

Directions:

Switch on the oven, set it to 325 degrees F and let preheat. Meanwhile, place all the ingredients in a bowl, and stir until well combined and incorporated.

Pour the batter in a loaf pan, greased with oil, and then bake the bread for 45 minutes or until bread has cooked.

Let the bread cool in its pan for 10 minutes, then take it out, transfer it to a wire rack to cool completely, then cut into 12 slices and serve.

Nutrition:

191 Cal
16 g Fats
5 g Protein
3 g Net Carb
3 g Fiber

Chocolate Chip Ricotta Bread

Preparation Time: 30-45 minutes

Cooking Time: 1 hour 30 minutes

Servings: 18

Ingredients: 2 eggs, pastured
1 1/2 cups almond flour, blanched
4 medium bananas, mashed
2 teaspoons baking powder
1 cup ricotta cheese, full-fat
1 cup chocolate chips, unsweetened
2 teaspoons vanilla extract, unsweetened

Directions: Switch on the oven, set it to 350 degrees F and let preheat. Meanwhile, place the mashed banana in a bowl, beat in vanilla, eggs, and cheese until combined and then beat in flour, salt, and baking powder until incorporated. Fold in chocolate chips, pour the mixture into a 9 by 5 inches loaf pan, lined with parchment sheet and bake the bread for 40 to 50 minutes or until the bread has cooked and an inserted toothpick into the bread comes out clean. Let the bread cool in the pan, then take it out, cut into 18 slices, and serve.

Nutrition: 121 Cal 9.8 g Fats 4.6 g Protein 2 g Net Carb 2.2 g Fiber

Butternut Squash Banana Bread

Preparation Time: 30-45 minutes

Cooking Time: 1 hour 30 minutes

Servings: 10

Ingredients:

1 3/4 cups almond flour, blanched

1 1/4 cup erythritol sweetener

2 tablespoons coconut flour

1/2 teaspoon salt

1 tablespoon and 1 teaspoon pumpkin pie spice

4 ounces cream cheese, softened

1/2 teaspoon vanilla extract, unsweetened

1/4 cup butter, unsalted, softened

2 eggs, pastured

1 cup pumpkin puree

For The Frosting:

1/2 teaspoon cinnamon

1/2 teaspoon vanilla extract, unsweetened

1/2 cup erythritol sweetener

4 ounces cream cheese, full-fat, softened

2 tablespoons butter, unsalted

Directions:

Switch on the oven, set it to 350 degrees F and let preheat. Meanwhile, place cream cheese in a bowl, add butter and sweetener, beat until creamy, beat in eggs, one at a time, and then beat in pumpkin puree and vanilla until mixed.

Stir together flours, salt and pumpkin pie spice in a bowl, slowly stir into the egg mixture until smooth and incorporated and then pour into a greased 9 by 5 inches loaf pan.

Bake the bread for 45 minutes until the bread has cooked and an inserted skewer into the bread comes out clean. Meanwhile, prepare the frosting and for this, beat together cream cheese and butter until creamy, then beat in cinnamon and vanilla, stir in sweetener and set aside until required.

When the bread has baked, let the bread cool for 10 minutes, then take it out, and transfer the bread on a wire rack to cool completely.

Spread the frosting on the bread, then cut into ten slices and serve.

Nutrition:

173 Cal

13 g Fats

6 g Protein

2.3 g Net Carb

1.3 g Fiber

Cranberry Orange Bread

Preparation Time: 30-45 minutes

Cooking Time: 1 hour 30 minutes

Servings: 12

Ingredients:

1 cup chopped fresh cranberries

9 tablespoons coconut flour

1 1/2 teaspoon baking powder

3 tablespoons Monk fruit powder

1/4 teaspoon salt

9 tablespoons butter, unsalted, melted

1 teaspoon vanilla extract, unsweetened
2/3 cup erythritol sweetener
1 1/2 teaspoon orange extract, unsweetened
5 eggs, pastured
1 egg yolk, pastured
2 tablespoons sour cream
For the Glaze:
2 tablespoons Monk fruit powder
1/2 tablespoon butter, unsalted, melted
1 teaspoon heavy whipping cream, grass-fed, full-fat

Directions:
Switch on the oven, set it to 350 degrees F and let preheat. Meanwhile, add eggs and egg yolks in a bowl and beat in erythritol, vanilla, butter, sour cream, and orange extract until combined and then beat in flour, salt, and baking powder until incorporated. Stir together cranberries and 3 tablespoons Monk fruit powder until coated, then fold into the prepared batter and pour into a loaf pan lined with parchment paper.
Bake the bread for 50 to 55 minutes or until the bread has cooked and an inserted skewer into the bread slides out clean. Meanwhile, prepare the glaze and for this, beat together butter, Monk fruit sweetener, and cream until mixture reach to the consistency of thick glaze, set aside until required. When the bread has cooked, top it with prepared glaze, let the bread cool for 15 minutes,

then cut into 12 slices and serve.
Nutrition:
139 Cal
12 g Fats
3 g Protein
2 g Net Carb
2 g Fiber

Bread Rolls

Preparation Time: 30-45 minutes
Cooking Time: 1 hour 30 minutes
Servings: 8

Ingredients:
1 1/2 cups shredded mozzarella cheese, full-fat
2 ounces cream cheese, full-fat
1 1/3 cups almond flour, blanched
2 tablespoons coconut flour
1 1/2 tablespoon baking powder
3 large eggs, pastured

Directions:
Switch on the oven, set it to 350 degrees F and let preheat. Meanwhile, stir together flours and baking powder until combined and set aside until required.

Place cream cheese and mozzarella cheese in a heatproof bowl, let microwave for 1 minute or until cheese melts, stirring every 30 seconds, and then let cool for 5 minutes until cool enough to handle.

Add flour mixture into a food processor, along with cold cheese and 2 eggs and pulse at high speed until the dough comes together.

Transfer the dough onto a large sheet, cover with a plastic wrap, then knead for 3 minutes until smooth and divide it into eight sections. Shape each section of dough to form a smooth ball and then place them on a baking sheet, about 2 inches apart. Whisk the remaining egg, brush it generously on dough balls and then bake in the middle rack of the preheated oven for 21 to 23 minutes until nicely golden brown. Serve hot.

Nutrition: 216 Cal
16 g Fats
11 g Protein
4 g Net Carb
2 g Fiber

Oopsie Rolls

Preparation Time: 30-45 minutes
Cooking Time: 1 hour 30 minutes
Servings: 6

Ingredients:
3 eggs, pastured, separated
1/8 teaspoon salt
1/8 teaspoon cream of tartar, full-fat
3 ounces cream cheese, full-fat, softened

Directions:
Switch on the oven, set it to 300 degrees F and let preheat. Meanwhile, place egg whites in a bowl, add cream of tartar and whip until stiff.

Place egg yolks in another bowl, add salt and cream cheese and whisk until smooth.

Fold in egg whites mixture in batches until incorporated, then take a cookie sheet, line it with parchment paper and

spoon the egg whites mixture in six mounds. Flatten each mound with a spatula and bake for 30 minutes or until the loaves of bread are nicely golden brown. Let the loaves of bread cool in the cookie sheet for 10 minutes, then cool completely on a wire rack and serve.
Nutrition:
91.3 Cal
8.1 g Fats
4.2 g Protein
0.8 g Net Carb
0 g Fiber

Russian Krendl Bread

Preparation Time: 45 minutes
Cooking Time: 45 minutes
Servings: Makes 24 servings
Ingredients:
One packet of (1/4 ounce) active dry yeast
Three tablespoons of sugar
3/4 cup warm half-and - a-half cream or whole milk (110 ° to 115 °)
1/4 cup butter, softened
Two big egg yolks
1-1/2 teaspoon vanilla extract
1/2 teaspoon salt
2-3/4 to 3-1/4 cup all-purpose flour
Filling:
1 cup of apple juice
One big apple, peeled and chopped
2/3 cup of finely chopped dried apples
1/3 cup of finely chopped dried apricots

1/3 cup of chopped dried pitted prunes
Five tablespoons of butter
Four tablespoons of sugar
1/2 teaspoon of ground cinnamon
Confectioners' sugar
Directions:
Dissolve the yeast and sugar in a small bowl in liquid water. Combine softened butter, egg yolks, cinnamon, salt, yeast mixture and 1-1/2 cup flour in a wide bowl beat at medium velocity until smooth. Add enough remaining flour to form a soft dough (the dough is sticky). Turn the dough onto a floured surface knead for around 6-8 minutes, until smooth and elastic. Place them in a greased tub, turning to graze the top once. Cover with plastic wrap and allow to rise until doubled in a warm spot for around 1 hour. Combine orange, apple, dried fruits, two tablespoons butter, and two tablespoons of sugar in a large saucepan for filling. Take to simmer. Reduce heat boil, expose, for 25-30 minutes or stir periodically until mixture reaches a jam-like consistency. Switch to a bowl, completely cool off. Punch the dough in. Turn onto a floured surface roll into a 32x10-in sheet— appropriate point. Melt the remaining butter

scatter over the dough to 1 in of rims. Mix the remaining cinnamon and sugar sprinkle over the edges—spread mixture with fruit. Roll up jelly-roll style, starting with a long side pinch seam and seal ends. Place seam side down on a baking sheet that is greased turn into a pretzel shape. Cover with a kitchen towel let it rise until almost doubled in a warm spot for about 30 minutes. The oven should be preheated to 350 ° C. Bake for 40-45 minutes or until golden brown. Remove from pan to cool wire rack at the time of serving, dust with confectioner's sugar.
Nutrition:
1 slice: 146 Calories,
6 g fat
31 mg cholesterol
92 mg sodium
21 g carbohydrate (9 g carbohydrates, 1 g fiber)
2 g protein

Flexseed Bread
Preparation time: 30 minutes
Cooking time: 45 minutes
Servings: approx.8 (2 slices per serving)
Ingredients:
2 cups flax seeds, ground
5 Eggs
½ cup water

5 1/3 tbsp butter or coconut butter, melted
1 tbsp baking powder
½ tsp sea salt
1 tbsp sesame, for sprinkling
Directions:
Heat the oven to 175°C.
Grind flax seeds on a coffee grinder.
In a deep bowl, whip the eggs+ salt + water.
Add the ground flax seeds, baking powder. Stir everything.

Add coconut or butter and mix to a homogeneous consistency.
Put the dough into a pre-greased baking dish.
Bake for 45 minutes at 175C.
Nutrition:
265 Calories per serving
Carbs 12g
fats 19.1g,
proteins 9.5g.

Chapter 16 Include some ideas for various shapes

For shaping, that's quite an easy thing to do. Kindly roll up the dough and place it on the length of your pan. Allow filling the containers the distance you want. Ensure you have a dry mixture as it's easier. If this is not the case, shaping a wet dough has to be carried out with caution and intelligence.

As you are removing the gas, shake and punch down, so they all come out. There is no fixed amount of gas to be evicted. You need to find what's right for you. When you achieve this, you will see and notice a good, even and tight bread on the inside.

So when you do not adequately degas, you are not helping some of the yeast feed more and give you their best result.

If you know how to apply the right amount of pressure using your hands, then welcome to the baker's world. There is no hard-fast rule about it, but be smart and always have an expected end in mind.

You can make different size breads in bread machine depending on which pan size you are using. There are three sizes of loaf pans that you can use: 1 pound, 1 ½ pound and 2 pounds.

1 pound is for smaller bread loafs for 8-10 bread slices.

The most common and popular size is 1 ½ pound. It makes standard size loaf with 12 slices.

2-pound loaf is for making larger loaf. It makes around 16 slices.

There are a lot of shapes that you can make for your bread circles, squares, heart shape, star, etc. anything that pops up on your creativity.

Shapes are also important because it gives beauty and art unto the bread itself. Honestly, bread is much fun to eat with when there is a little bit of art to it.

Circle Shape
Heart Shape
Star Shape
Square Shape
House Shape
Crescent Shape
Diamond Shape

And many more, as long as you put your creativity upon it, it will surely result to a beautiful and attractive master piece.
Tip: Do not be plain, use some icing, butter, candies, sprinkles, milk, etc.

Mixing

Mixing the ingredients is easier when using an electric mixer. But, mixing by hand is also possible. It may just take more time and energy. Don't be discouraged when you find that your mixture doesn't seem to come together, it'll get better once you start kneading.

Kneading

After mixing all the bread ingredients, knead it to make the dough elastic and smooth. Some of the bread recipes in this book won't require kneading because of their fluid-like consistency. It would take 5-10 minutes depending on the recipe. After kneading, your dough should hold its shape together.

Shaping the dough

You also need to learn how to shape the dough depending on the type of bread you're making. You may need bread-shaping tools to shape the dough correctly.

Making a single loaf of bread may require the use of multiple bowls, pots, pans, and utensils, all of which need to be washed and put away. It is also difficult to make bread without flour falling on the entire countertop and often on the floor. And this mess must also be cleared up. But you don't have to worry if you use a bread machine. Everything that can lead to disorder takes place inside the machine. Apart from the bread maker, you only have to clean one or two measuring cups. Don't worry about mistakes. There is a lot of stuff that can go wrong if you make bread entirely by hand. You couldn't knead the dough enough. Or you knead the dough too much. Or you could make a mistake with the yeast and not let the dough rise properly. Any of these adversities can result in bread that is hard, tough. Fortunately, using a bread machine makes bread almost foolproof. You don't have to care about how much dough to knead or whether the bread dough will rise or not. The machine does all of this for you. Now that you know the benefits of a bread machine, it's time to choose one that suits you.

Baking with a bread machine can be a real pleasure, but the sheer number of cycles and settings can be confusing. Many early bakers are not sure what the different names actually mean. Those of you who don't have the manual or bought your machine second-hand may need a little help with the basics. This list is intended to help you navigate through the most common settings and cycles of modern bread machines. Although bread machines are generally easy to use unless you know what the different cycles and settings mean, you can still experience a disaster instead of a masterpiece. However, the explanations above are intended to help you become more familiar with your device. Even if you don't have a manual on hand, this should make it easier for you to get started. Have fun baking! First of all, the main advantage of a bread machine is that you can relax a little while baking bread at the same time. Yes, it is true! Believe it or not, on some machines, you just have to add all the ingredients, and then it is the one who does what is left.

Chapter 17 Recommend ingredients to eat with bread

Blueberry Ice Cream

Preparation time: 10 minutes
Cooking time: 30 minutes
Servings: 6

Ingredients:
Blueberry Puree
2 cups blueberries, fresh or frozen
2 tbsp lemon juice
1 tbsp water
1/3 cup granulated erythritol or erythritol blend
1/8 tsp ground cinnamon
1/8 tsp almond extract
1/2 tsp vanilla extract
Ice Cream Base
1 cup almond milk, unsweetened
2 cups heavy cream
1/2 cup granulated erythritol
2 tbsp vodka
1/4 tsp table salt

Directions:
To Make the Blueberry Puree
Add blueberries, water, lemon juice, cinnamon, and sweetener to a saucepan.
Cover the berries and cook on low heat for 10 minutes.
Mix well then puree the berries until smooth.
Return the mixture to the saucepan and cook for another 20 minutes until it thickens.
To Make the Ice Cream Base
Add vodka, salt, sweetener, cream, and almond milk to a blender.
Pulse and blend well until combined.
Stir in the blueberry puree and blend well.
Transfer the blueberry mixture to an ice cream maker and churn as per the machine's instructions.
Freeze until it's firm then serve.
Nutrition:
Calories 254
Total Fat 9 g
Saturated Fat 10.1 g
Cholesterol 13 mg
Sodium 179 mg
Total Carbs 7.5 g
Sugar 1.2 g
Fiber 0.8 g
Protein 7.5 g

Matcha Ice Cream

Preparation time: 10 minutes
Freeze time: 3 hours
Servings: 2

Ingredients:
1 cup heavy cream
1 tsp matcha powder
2 tbsp monk fruit, Swerve
1/2 tsp vanilla extract

Directions:
Start by throwing all the ingredients into a mason jar.
Shake it all well for 5 minutes then freeze for 3 hours.
Serve.
Nutrition:
Calories 290
Total Fat 21.5 g
Saturated Fat 15.2 g

Cholesterol 12.1 mg
Sodium 9 mg
Total Carbs 6.5 g
Sugar 1.2 g
Fiber 0.4 g
Protein 6.2 g

Cook the cauliflower for 2
minutes on Manual mode at
High pressure.
Once soft, add cauliflower and
water to a food processor.
Blend well then add the
remaining ingredients.
Blend again until smooth then
refrigerate for 3 hours.
Serve.
Nutrition:
Calories 214
Total Fat 19 g
Saturated Fat 5.8 g
Cholesterol 15 mg
Sodium 123 mg
Total Carbs 6.5 g
Sugar 1.9 g
Fiber 2.1 g
Protein 6.5 g

Cauliflower Chocolate Pudding

Preparation time: 10 minutes
Cooking Time: 3 hours
Servings: 6

Ingredients:
16 oz cauliflower florets
½ cup of water
5 tbsp raw cacao powder
3-5 tbsp maple syrup
2 tbsp MCT oil
10-15 drops liquid vanilla
stevia
½ tsp vanilla extract
1/4-½ tsp salt

Directions:
Start by adding water to an
Instant Pot and seal its lid.

Flavored Chia Pudding

Preparation time: 10 minutes
Cooking time: 1 hour
Total time: 1 hour 10 minutes
Servings: 2

Ingredients:

1/3 cup chia seeds
1 ½ cups unsweetened almond milk
1/2 cup heavy whipping cream
2 tsp banana flavoring
1 tsp vanilla extract
1 tbsp erythritol

Directions:

Add all the liquid into a jar adding the chia seeds last.
Mix well with a fork and cover it.
Refrigerate for 1 hour then garnish with coconut chips, chocolate chips, almonds, and berries.
Serve.

Nutrition:
Calories 282
Total Fat 25.1 g
Saturated Fat 8.8 g
Cholesterol 100 mg
Sodium 117 mg
Total Carbs 9.4 g
Sugar 0.7 g
Fiber 3.2 g
Protein 8 g

Mint Chia Pudding

Preparation time: 10 minutes
Cooking Time: Overnight
(plus overnight refrigeration)
Servings: 2

Ingredients:

¾ cup almond milk
¼ tsp vanilla extract
¼ tsp peppermint extract
2 tbsp chia seeds
2 tbsp dark chocolate chips

Directions:

Add almond milk, peppermint extract, chia seeds, and vanilla extract to a bowl.
Mix and cover it with plastic wrap then refrigerate it overnight.
Garnish with chocolate chips.
Serve.

Nutrition:
Calories 331
Total Fat 38.5 g
Saturated Fat 19.2 g
Cholesterol 141 mg
Sodium 283 mg
Total Carbs 9.2 g
Sugar 3 g

Fiber 1 g
Protein 2.1 g

Lemon Cheesecake Mousse

Preparation time: 10 minutes
Cooking time: 0 minutes
Servings: 2
Ingredients:
8 oz cream cheese, room temperature
1 cup heavy cream, cold
2/3 cup lemon curd
1/3 cup Swerve confectioners
Directions:
Beat cream in a bowl until it forms peaks.
Separately, beat cream cheese using a hand mixer then add the lemon curd and Swerve in a mixer.
Stir in the whipped cream then refrigerate for 10 minutes.
Garnish as desired.
Serve.
Nutrition:
Calories 267
Total Fat 44.5 g
Saturated Fat 17.4 g
Cholesterol 153 mg
Sodium 217 mg
Total Carbs 8.4 g

Sugar 2.3 g
Fiber 1.3 g
Protein 3.1 g

Creamy Ricotta Coffee Mousse

Preparation time: 10 minutes
Cooking time: 3 hours
Servings: 6
Ingredients:
2 cups ricotta cheese
1 cup heavy cream, chilled
1/3 cup monk fruit sweetener
1 1/2 tbsp instant espresso powder
1 tbsp powdered gelatin
For Whipped Cream Topping
1 cup heavy cream, chilled
1/3 cup monk fruit sweetener
1 tsp gelatin
1 tbsp orange zest, finely grated
Shaved chocolate, for garnish
Directions:
Add ricotta to a blender and blend until smooth.
Beat 1 cup heavy cream with 1/3 cup sweetener in a mixer until it forms peaks.
Heat 1/4 cup water in a saucepan to boil then mix 2 tablespoons of this water with gelatin.
Mix well then set this mixture aside.
Mix ricotta with espresso, gelatin mixture, and whipped cream.
Divide this dessert into 6 serving glasses then refrigerate for 1 hour.
Beat a cup of cream with 1/3 cup sweetener, 2 tablespoons

water, and 1 teaspoon gelatin in a bowl.
Place this bowl in the microwave and heat the cream mixture for 1 minute.
Beat well then fold in orange zest then transfer the mixture to a piping bag.
Pipe this mixture over the coffee mouse.
Refrigerate for 2 hours then garnish with chocolate shavings.
Serve.
Nutrition:
Calories 259
Total Fat 34 g
Saturated Fat 10.3 g
Cholesterol 112 mg
Sodium 92 mg
Total Carbs 8.5 g
Sugar 2 g
Fiber 1.3 g
Protein 7.5 g

Mix well then fold in egg whites.
Divide this batter into the serving bowls.
Serve.
Nutrition:
Calories 255
Total Fat 23.4 g
Saturated Fat 11.7 g
Cholesterol 135 mg
Sodium 112 mg
Total Carbs 2.5 g
Sugar 12.5 g
Fiber 1 g
Protein 7.9 g

Frozen Raspberry Mousse

Preparation time: 10 minutes
Cooking time: 0 minutes
Servings: 2
Ingredients:
3 egg whites
2 cups raspberries, fresh
1 tbsp vodka or rum
1/2 cup Swerve
Directions:
Start by blending the 3 egg whites in a blender until foamy and set aside.
Separately, blend the raspberries in a blender then add ½ cup sweetener and vodka/rum.

Pumpkin Cheesecake Mousse

Preparation time: 10 minutes
Cooking time: 2 hours
Servings: 4

Ingredients:
8 oz cream cheese, softened
1 cup canned pumpkin puree
1/2 cup Swerve sweetener
1 tsp pumpkin pie spice
1 tsp vanilla extract
3/4 cup heavy whipping cream

Directions:
Start by adding cream cheese and pumpkin puree to a mixing bowl.
Mix until smooth then stir in remaining ingredients.
Transfer the mixture to a piping bag.
Pipe this mixture into small cups.
Refrigerate for 2 hours.

Serve.
Nutrition:
Calories 251
Total Fat 24.5 g
Saturated Fat 14.7 g
Cholesterol 165 mg
Sodium 142 mg
Total Carbs 4.3 g
Sugar 0.5 g
Fiber 1 g
Protein 5.9 g

Chapter 18 Common mistakes in baking bread

Many problems can occur during the baking of the bread in the machine if you do not know how to use it properly. Here are some common mistakes that usually happen and tips to avoid them.

- **The crust is too thick and dark**

This usually happens because the bread has been left in the machine for too long after the baking is completed. To fix the problem, you have to remove the bread immediately after it is done.

- **Bread collapsing out of the machine**

This happens when your yeast does not react properly with the rest of the ingredients. It could be the temperature or the problem of the ingredients. To ensure that this never happens, accurately take the temperature of the ingredients. Use enough liquids, not too much. Some people use a lot of yeast, so use less amount of yeast in baking. You can also add more salt. During a season of high humidity and warmth, use less amount of and cooler liquids.

- **Bread not rising at all even during baking**

This can happen for multiple reasons. To fix this problem, accurately measure the number of ingredients. This can also be caused by using low gluten flour. You need to check if your yeast works or not. Also, you need to check the temperature of the liquids.

- **Bread being too dense**

This can occur if you're using whole grains instead of white flour. Keep checking the moisture so that it's not too dry. If you are using low gluten flour, your bread will not be stable enough, so you need to add more gluten.

- **Bread is raw in the center**

This can happen if you use too much liquid in your mix. You also need to check your yeast's activity. This can also happen if the bread machine is not working properly. You can check your manuals instructions to figure that out.

- **No color on top**

You need to add an adequate amount of sugar to have good color. Use too much, and it will be too dark. It could be that you're using too many ingredients, so use a smaller recipe. If your machine has a glass top, put foil on the lid.

To follow is a list of the most common problems and solutions when baking bread using a bread machine.

Problem:
* The dough does not rise.

Possible Cause:
* The liquid added was too hot or too cold. It should be tepid between 20-25 °C/68-77°F.
* Not enough yeast was added. Make sure your measurements are accurate.
* Yeast was not fresh and therefore inactive.
* Yeast came into contact with salt prior to mixing.
* Too much salt was added counteracting performance of yeast. Make sure your measurements are accurate.

Problem:
* Bread has risen and fallen over the side of the loaf tin.

Possible Cause:
* Too much dough. Check you have selected the right quantity of ingredients for your loaf and bread machine.
* Too much yeast has caused the bread to over-rise. Make sure your measurements are accurate.
* Not enough sugar. Make sure your measurements are accurate.
* Not enough salt. Salt affects the performance of yeast, too little or too much will have an adverse effect on your loaf.

Problem:
* Bread has collapsed.

Possible Cause:
* Too much yeast has caused the bread to over-rise. Make sure your measurements are accurate.

Problem:
* Bread is heavy.

Possible Cause:
* Not enough liquid.
* Too much flour.
* Flour or yeast is not fresh. Make sure ingredients are fresh and quantities are accurate.

Problem:
* Bread is very dry.

Possible Cause:
* Not enough liquid. Make sure your measurements are accurate.

* If your loaf contains oats, bran, rye or wholegrains it may be that they have soaked up additional liquid. Experiment by adding slightly more liquid or reduce the quantity of grains.
Problem:
* Bread is undercooked in the middle.
Possible Cause:
* Not enough flour.
* Too much liquid.
* Flour is of a poor quality or is not fresh.
Problem:
* Bread crust is burnt.
Possible Cause:
* Too much sugar. Reduce quantity of sugar or sugar-based ingredients. You may also consider using the sweet bread cycle if your machine has one, which will bake your bread at a lower temperature and therefore avoid burning the crust.
* Dark crust has been selected. Select a lighter crust setting.
Problem:
* Crust is not crispy.
Possible Cause:
* Loaf requires a French bread cycle if your machine has one.
* Loaf requires milk to replace water quantity.
If you are new to baking with a bread machine, you might have some problems at first using the device. Here are some helpful tips to get your bread baking days started without a hassle.

- Add or layer the ingredients into the machine according to the company's instruction manual. It has steps and guidance written down for almost every situation.

- Use room temperature water when adding and not too hot or too cold. It should be around 80°F or 26°C.

- Use fresh ingredients as much as possible. You can add dry ingredients at room temperature.

- If you are new to using the bread machine, it's better to experiment with bread flour at first. Make a few loaves of bread using it to get a feel for what is right and what doesn't work. Bread flour is stronger than other flour, and it will resist the machine's processing.

- Use active dry yeast when making bread in regular cycles. Do not use active dry yeast on express cycles or one-hour cycles. You can generally use ¾ tablespoon of yeast for every cup of flour.

- Use instant yeast according to the settings provided by the company. You generally have to add half tablespoon of yeast for every cup of flour. You may have to double that amount for Express or one-hour cycles. Temperature also differs from machine-to-machine, so follow the guidelines carefully.
- Make sure that the yeast is fresh
- otherwise, the bread will not rise. To check if it's fresh, do a proofing test.
- When placing the yeast in the machine, make a shallow depression in the dough and place it there. Do not directly put on salt or sugar
- this will decrease the yeast's action.
- It is important to check the dough's moisture. A few minutes into the kneading cycle, open to check if the door is in the consistently that you want. If it's too wet, add flour, and if it's too dry, add milk or water.
- If the milk is included in the ingredients and you have to use the delayed cycle, replace it with buttermilk or powder milk.
- If you're adding butter or margarine into the mix, first cut them into pieces and then add them into the machine.
- You must measure flour carefully. Use a tablespoon to put the flour into the measuring cup, once full, gently slide your finger across the surface. This will ensure good measuring.

Chapter 19 Bread storage

Storing your bread is fairly simple and can be done anytime you make your bread. Store the items in the freezer or anywhere in your refrigerator. Sandwich loaves should be sliced before freezing. You can always just take out what you can eat, and store the rest for later in your refrigerator. Cooling your loaves after baking is very essential if you plan on freezing the bread, make sure it has completed its cool down cycle. Slice and add it to freezer bags remove all of the excessive air.

Bread machine bread is so delicious, you might create more than you, your family, and your friends can eat in one sitting. Here are some tips for storing your bread machine creations:

Dough. After the kneading cycle, remove the dough from the machine. If you plan on using the dough within three days, you can store it in the refrigerator. Form the dough into a disk and place it in a sealable freezer bag, or store the dough in a lightly oiled bowl covered with plastic wrap. Yeast action will not stop in the refrigerator, so punch the dough down until it is completely chilled, and then once a day. When you are ready to bake bread, remove the dough from the refrigerator, shape it, let it rise, and bake. Bread machine dough has no preservatives, so freeze it if you aren't baking it in three days. Form the dough into a disk and place it in a sealable freezer bag. You can freeze bread dough for up to a month. When you are ready to bake the bread, remove the dough from the freezer, store it in the refrigerator overnight, shape it, let it rise, and bake. You can shape the dough into braids, loaves, knots, or other shapes before refrigerating or freezing it. Wrap the shapes tightly and store in the refrigerator (if you are baking within 24 hours) or the freezer. At the right time, unwrap the dough, allow it to rise at room temperature, and bake it.

Baked Bread. Once your baked bread is cooled, wrap the loaf in plastic wrap or a freezer bag and place it in the refrigerator or freezer. You can freeze baked bread for up to 6 months. To thaw the bread, remove it from the freezer, unwrap the loaf partially, and let it sit at room temperature. If you want to serve warm bread after refrigerating or freezing a loaf, wrap the bread in aluminum foil, and bake it in an oven preheated to 300°F for 10 to 15 minutes.

Try not to believe that homemade bread should keep insofar as commercially made assortments. In our home, newly cooked bread is probably not going to keep going long at any rate

thus, when it has cooled totally, I store it in a bread canister in the kitchen.

Specialists keep up that the ideal approach to store bread is to wrap it firmly in foil or seal it in a plastic pack and keep it at room temperature. Continuously oppose the impulse to refrigerate bread on the grounds that staling is at its generally fast in normal cooler temperatures.

If you truly need to keep bread for longer than a day or two, the ideal route is to freeze it. Except for extremely dried up loaves, most crisp bread can be solidified for around about a month wrapped and fixed in freezer packs. At the point when you need to eat it, enable the bread to defrost (still in its sack) at room temperature or defrost it on an exceptionally low force in the microwave. If you utilize just limited quantities of bread, it is a smart thought to cut bread before freezing and take it out a couple of pieces one after another.

Now that you have all this wonderful homemade bread, how can you store it to keep it fresh? Believe it or not, freezing your bread is the best option. Bread can be stored up to 2 months in a freezer, and warned up as needed. If you are planning on eating your bread soon after baking, leaving it out uncovered is one way to go. Even if the crust gets a little hard the inside should be fine.

An old-fashioned way to keep bread around longer is storing it in a bread box. This way the bread is covered and unexposed to air. Bread can also be wrapped in plastic to preserve it, just ensure that it's placed in a cool, dry area with no moisture. Whatever you decide to do, do not put fresh bread in the refrigerator, because it will become dried out.

We do not want to waste every single piece of bread we made, we want to share them to others, and have it 'til supper and whatnot. Therefore, do not let your bread goes out of freshness, store bread properly, always follow the guidelines. Enjoy your baking.

Chapter 20 Storage of the remaining bread

Storing bread isn't always easy. If you manage not to eat all of the delicious goodies that you bake, you should find the best ways to store them so that you can keep them fresh longer. There are plenty of different things to keep in mind when it comes to storing bread, but homemade bread is especially delicate. Here are some tips to help you get the most out of your storage:

Don't store bread in the refrigerator. While this might seem like the freshness solution, it actually changes the alignment of the starch molecules, which is what causes bread to go stale. If you have leftovers from what you have baked, keep it on the counter or in the bread box.

Make sure that you don't leave bread sitting out for too long. Once you cut into a loaf, you have a limited amount of time to wrap it up and secure the freshness inside. If the interior is exposed to the air for too long, it will start to harden and go stale much quicker.

If your home or the bread itself is warm, do not put it in a plastic bag. The warmth will encourage condensation, which will prompt mold growth in the warm, moist environment. Wait until bread cools completely before storing it.

Pre-sliced and store-bought bread are going to go bad much quicker, simply because of all of the exposure and additives (which, ironically, are sometimes to retain freshness). If you're making your own bread with your bread machine, and you manage to have leftovers, these tips will make sure that you get the most out of your bread.

*Moisture Matters

Just as with the baking process, the humidity and moisture in your home will affect the lifespan of your bread. It will also affect the storage options that you have. If the weather is more humid, you could leave bread on the counter overnight. However, it may have a softer crust as a result. Too much humidity means you need to store your bread in airtight containers and remove as much air and moisture as you can before storage.

That means letting the bread cool to room temperature before putting into plastic bags or containers. You will also want to hold off on slicing your bread when it first comes out of the bread machine. Unless you are going to eat the entire loaf within a short period of time, the best plan is to wait. When you cut into warm bread, steam comes out. That steam is moisture, which is helping the bread stay fresh and delicious. If you cut it too soon, you'll lose that freshness.

If you leave bread out on the counter and it is too dry, it will quickly turn into a brick. The lack of humidity is too much for fresh bread, and even too much for most store-bought varieties. Moisture is a balance, and you have to find what works for your bread, and in your home. Remember that whole grain bread, French bread, and other harder bread will generally last much longer than soft sandwich bread. If you store your bread in plastic too soon or for too long, the crust will go soft, as we mentioned before. However, you can avoid this by leaving the bread on the counter or wrapping it loosely with a cloth or paper once it is cool. For crust lovers, this is crucial. It's all about figuring out what works in your home and with your tastes, so feel free to experiment with storage solutions, too.

*To Freeze Or Not To Freeze?

You CAN freeze your bread. However, you simply have to be sure that you are doing it the right way. First of all, make sure that the bread is cooled to room temperature and that you have a paper or cloth wrapped around it to help collect and retain the moisture. Seal it tightly or wrap it securely, and store away for up to six months. Ideally use a vacuum sealer to make sure the bread is completely sealed.

The difficulty in freezing bread and other baked goods is not actually in the freezing process, but the thawing. It is critical that you take the bread out of the freezer ahead of time. Rather than defrosting it in the microwave or oven, you need to let it thaw completely. This will allow the bread to re-absorb any moisture that it lost during the freezing process, keeping it fresh and delicious. Once the bread comes to room temperature, you can toss it in the oven for a few minutes to warm it up.

Reheating bread is tricky. Moisture is the biggest problem with reheating or storing bread, and freezing can affect that in many different ways. It is going to be up to you to figure out the best ways to store and reheat your bread, but these tips should definitely help.

*Other Storage Solutions

There is also the option of the bread box. Many bakers have been using these for centuries, and although they aren't as popular now as they were 20 years ago, they do still exist. Is a bread box the right choice for your bread? Consider a few things:

The type of material the box is made of. Metal versus wood boxes makes a big difference. It might also affect the storage and shelf-life based on other elements.

What type of bread are you storing? All breads are different and react differently when stored. Make sure that you take the time to get to know your bread varieties, as well as what is best for them.

Chapter 21 Some advice

When you first start to make bread, you may expect to just put the ingredients inside the pan and let the bread maker do the rest. While this is an entirely reasonable way to start making bread, it's good to start learning some of the tricks of the trade to get the best bread in your neighborhood.

Start Simple

It should come as no surprise that the best way to get your feet wet in the bread making machine world is to start with simple recipes. If your great-grandmother had the best bread in the world that was made with 25 spices and it takes over 24 hours to make, do not be surprised if your first attempt does not yield proper results. Try no-brainer recipes and breads that are easy to complete and involve few ingredients. Even the recipes in bread maker booklets sometimes do not work. Your skills improve as you adjust the ingredients to your liking and find out what works best.

As the Internet has grown, great sites, such as Pinterest, have places to keep your recipes to try over and over. Take your time getting used to the machine before you try breads not normally cooked in a bread maker. Every machine is different, so get used to yours before you move to more complicated recipes.

Be Cautious About Substitutions

Bread makers are especially susceptible to slight changes in recipes. Something as little as a change in the type of flour you use could result in bread completely different than what you made before. That is because all flours have different gluten ratios and density. For example, you may find that you have denser bread when you use all-purpose flour as opposed to bread flour. Since bread is primarily made from flour, any small changes are noticeable.

Also, consider what yeast you use in your recipes. If the recipe calls for instant yeast, do not substitute it with regular yeast. Yeast is one of the most difficult parts of bread making to get right. First, you must find the correct temperature for the yeast to grow. Anything too hot will kill all the yeast cells, and anything too cold will make them remain dormant. This is why yeast is commonly kept refrigerated. Recipes also generally include the brand of yeast they used in their recipes. If you can, try to find the same products.

Don't be Afraid to Peek

Perhaps the most important advice here is to always monitor your bread. Bread machines have windows for a reason, but you may not be able to see the churning dough within. Besides, as the yeast grows, condensation builds up at the top of the machine, blocking your view. It is certainly not bad to open the lid to take a look in fact, that is what you should do with every baking project.

Paddles may come off of their rotators, rendering them useless. If half of your loaf is a brown mess while the other half holds some promise, it is likely that your paddle has been removed. So, about ten minutes into the bread machine cycle, check to make sure that everything is rotating smoothly. Make sure that the paddles click into their designated spots and continue to turn. Many a bread maker has felt the sting of finding no blade when they reach their hands down inside of the machine.

Check the consistency of the dough at about 10 minutes to see how everything is forming. If your dough is too wet, it will not cook properly, and it will become crumbly and soggy. If the dough appears goopy and has no grip on the other parts of the dough, it can be fixed. To fix this problem, slowly add flour to the mixture, one tablespoon at a time. On the flip side, bread dough may mix to become far too dry. The dough stays at the center of the bread machine and does not touch the edges. To fix this, add water in tablespoon increments to the machine. Perfect dough should stick to the sides of the pan but also form a ball.

Check on the bread frequently as well. Though it is often unwise to open the lid frequently when the bread machine is baking, it never hurts to get a sneak peek of how the dough turns out. If you open the lid too often, however, the top will fall, and your bread will not hold to the famous sandwich bread shape.

Try the Dough Cycle

Though it is the most convenient to just add the ingredients to a bread machine and let it take over from there, if you use the dough cycle instead of depending solely on letting the bread maker do all of your baking, you may see some amazing results. Some bread machine gurus rarely use the baking method. They prefer to style their bread in interesting patterns or top the bread with a glaze they simply will not receive from a bread machine.

One of the best parts of fresh bread is its crust. There are hundreds of styles of bread, and each of them requires different baking techniques. Some require different temperatures while others require detailed preparation of the dough before it is baked. The crusts created through the bread machine are often beautiful, but they lack advanced techniques to make them more delicious. Though bread makers have programs to make the changes, they cannot accommodate every style. Make the dough with a bread maker, but try using an oven for the rest of the work.

Depending on the type of bread machine you purchase, there are several kinds of dough cycles from which to choose. You can allow your bread to rise within the bread machine, or you can simply create the dough and do all the work of rising yourself. Though it may take a purist to only allow the machine do the mixing, there are some people who only want the dough to be mixed thoroughly and with the right consistency. For everyone else, use the quick cycle to make dough and let it rise within the machine.

If you have a machine that has the option of waiting until the bread cycle begins, make sure that your yeast is kept away from your liquids. You do not want your dough to grow before you have started the mixing process. Follow instructions to get the best results from your bread machine.

Knead Dough after Dough Cycle

Do not pound the living daylights out of dough that has just come out of the bread maker, but it is wise to knead the dough for a minute or two. By letting the dough rest, it becomes more pliable later. Even if you do not knead the dough for more than 30 seconds, you will see an improvement in your dough.

Do Not Flour the Surface

If you are using the dough technique when creating bread, consider forgoing the floured surface. Using too much flour will make your bread flaky and too dry, which will give you a bad final product. Instead, oil the surface of your counters when kneading dough. The extra oils that soak into the bread will not affect the overall quality of the bread negatively. In fact, if you coat your bread before it goes in the oven, you will find that the crust has a better texture. You may find that flavored oils add to the overall flavor of your bread. Make sure, though, that you are not using strange oils with exotic bread, because it will ruin the flavor.

Also, using oil prevents sticky bread dough from attaching to your fingers. If you have ever worked with wet dough, you know what we mean. The oils make both the bread and your hands slippery, so sticky dough will not catch.

Handle Dough Gently

After you have let the dough rest, take it out again and start to knead it. Use a gentle approach to maintain the surface tension on the bread that will yield a larger loaf. Gently push the dough flat against the kneading surface and fold a few times. Once finished, you can shape the dough into whatever designs you enjoy the most.

Keep the dough in a warm spot so it can rise sufficiently. Let it rise for about twenty minutes before checking to see if it has risen enough. Poke a finger into the dough if it bounces back and slowly slinks downward again, it is done. If you are new to baking, experiment with the results to find which works best for you. If you cannot finish with baking, stick the dough in the refrigerator for up to 24 hours. You will allow the yeast to hibernate as you wait for a time to complete the baking.

Cooking Measurement Conversion

US Dry Volume Measurements

1/16 teaspoon	a dash
1/8 teaspoon	a pinch
3 teaspoons	1 tablespoon
1/4 cup	4 tablespoons
1/3 cup	5 tablespoons + 1 teaspoon
1/2 cup	8 tablespoons
3/4 cup	12 tablespoons
1 cup	16 tablespoons
1 pound	16 ounces

US Liquid Volume Measurements

8 fluid ounces	1 cup
1 pint = 2 cups	16 fluid ounces
1 quart = 2 pints	4 cups
1 gallon = 4 quarts	16 cups

Conclusion

Bread machine has simplified the task of bread making like nothing. It spares you from spending hours just for preparations. I love making breads and bread machine has increased my cravings to try out more varieties at home because it is so easy now to bake fresh breads.

The book provides an exclusive collection of the best breads recipes to prepare using a bread machine. I am certain that versatile bread recipes covered in the book will help all its readers to learn making them at home and share with friend and loved ones.

Bread recipes offer great flexibility and freedom. You can make custom flavor breads by adding your choice of fresh fruits, vegetables, seeds, nuts, spices etc. and create new flavors of your own choice.

Now that you have completed this book, you are a pro, right? Well, you may not have the skills of a career bread maker, but you have certainly learned the basics. Some of the recipes in this book are designed to challenge you and get you thinking about how to make your own recipes. With the many functions of a bread machine, there is very little you cannot do.

Bread is one of the foundations of life. Almost any novel written with regard to an ancient prison will tell you that bread was the basis of survival. However, as times have changed, making bread at home has fallen by the wayside. However, our society claims bread is one of the best parts of any meal. So where has it gone?

Most bread now is manufactured in a factory and the products are sent directly to grocery stores in plastic bags instead of in paper sacks from bakeries. Though there are countries that still have a heavy reliance on bakeries, the United States sadly suffers. When you look at crafty sites, such as Pinterest, there are hundreds of recipes for bread, but there are few bakeries that have those variations. The sad truth is that everyone is becoming too busy to create culinary masterpieces. With a world on the go, it is often difficult to find time to babysit some dough that may require three hours of rising and another 40 minutes to bake. Bread machines, though, are the saving grace of a busy lifestyle.

Many bread machines today only require you to place the ingredients in the baking pan and click a setting for the bread. Suddenly, the four hours you may have spent sitting across from the oven has become an avenue for your escape. You can leave a bread machine for hours and let it do the work. Once it is done, most bread machines will keep your bread warm, but not burn it, so you can return to a home smelling of bliss.

Make sure that you pay close attention to the recipes when you first start to make bread. Almost all bread machines require some tweaking, so do not be disappointed if your loaf is not as pretty as the picture. The ingredients used in each recipe are vital to creating a great loaf. If you will notice, some recipes require more than one style of flour, and using the flour suggested just might save you the pain of defeat. People from across the globe have made bread a pastime and a symbol of self-expression, so when you have the basics down, start to experiment with your own ideas.

In this book, we promised that you would learn the best kinds of machines to buy and how different models would help you succeed in making different kinds of bread. We also promised that you would learn the tricks of the trade, using the advice of seasoned bread makers to make your bread pop. And finally, we promised that you would receive recipes for both regular and gluten-free options. This book is laid out to help you navigate through it again and again when you are unsure. All of the work in this book was created to make your bread-machine journey easier. Luckily, everything we promised has made it into the book.

Bread making with a bread machine is one of the best ways to save on money, save time on baking, and save your hard-earned money for other things. It is also a great way to get people together to enjoy some good food.

CPSIA information can be obtained
at www.ICGtesting.com
Printed in the USA
LVHW080852151120
671749LV00006B/75